I0783376

The Legacy of the Gray Winter

An Environmental Dystopian Disaster

MARTINA VIEIRA

Copyright © 2024 Martina Vieira

All rights reserved.

The characters and events portrayed in this book are fictitious. Any resemblance to actual persons, living or dead, is coincidental and not intended by the author.

ISBN: 9798302950543
Imprint: Independently Published

The true tragedy of human existence is that we possess the ability
to foresee our own downfall, yet lack the wisdom to prevent it
ANONYMOUS.

PROLOGUE

The year 2047 had transformed the cities of the Northern Hemisphere into bleak backdrops—a dystopia steadily creeping its way southward. In Plainfield, a typical Midwestern American city, extreme air pollution had radically altered daily life.

Streets, once bustling with life, now lay deserted and silent under a thick, gray smog that swallowed all color. A woman wearing a breathing mask coughed heavily as she hurriedly crossed the street, clutching a small child's hand. The little girl's bright red coat stood out starkly against the drab landscape, yet even this vibrant spot of color faded in the heavy fog. With tearful eyes, the child clung tightly to her mother, afraid of getting lost in the haze. The smog, so dense that visibility barely extended beyond two steps, made vehicle use virtually impossible. People consciously avoided using cars, following strict government orders to prevent air pollution from worsening, and the woman knew her only option was to catch the bus. Moments later, it emerged, ghostlike from the fog—driverless, powered by advanced GPS technology and equipped with automatic air filters. The bus registered their presence, and the doors opened with a quiet hiss. Quickly, the mother pushed her child inside and climbed in herself. A brief glance at the other passengers revealed blank, detached eyes staring silently out at the monochrome world beyond their masks.

The mother sat down. Her daughter climbed immediately on her lap. Together, they stared out at the hazy, desolate world stretching out endlessly before them. As the bus glided through the streets, the city unveiled itself in all its bleak splendor. Soot-covered facades lined the way, their windows sealed tightly to keep the toxic outside world at bay. Occasionally, delivery vehicles buzzed past, their filtration systems whirring as they brought a few essential goods to residents who scarcely ventured outside their homes anymore. An abandoned playground came into view—the swings swayed idly in the wind, the joyous laughter of children that once filled the air having long fallen quiet. The girl snuggled closer to her mother, her wide eyes desperately searching for some glimmer of comfort. "Everything will be alright," the mother whispered, gently stroking her daughter's hair.

As the bus passed a closed school building, the mother imagined the deserted classrooms. Schools had long since switched to digital instruction, as the journey to school had grown too dangerous for children. The empty rooms now seemed like remnants of a bygone era.

Lost in thought, her eyes drifted to the locked doors of what was once her favorite café. Then, it had been alive with warmth and joy; now, tables stood forlorn among dead trees in the empty garden. She closed her eyes, picturing herself there in better times, surrounded by people savoring life. A sharp pang pierced her heart as the memory overwhelmed her. She missed the aroma of freshly brewed coffee, the warmth of the sun on her skin, and the hearty laughter of her friends. Now, she only saw them through cold screens—a poor substitute for the closeness she so deeply craved. She tightened her scarf around herself as if it might shield her from the pervasive despair. The bus's monotonous hum blended in her head with the constant buzz emanating from the billions of devices worldwide, consuming energy and driving the demand for fossil fuels ever higher, thickening the smog. *A vicious cycle. Our digital escape accelerating our own undoing.*

As the bus continued through the abandoned city, her gaze

landed on a screen mounted high above the seats. The news anchor, with a somber expression, announced the latest failure of the global environmental summit. "Once again, no consensus in sight" were the only words she absorbed. The endless debates, the deaf ears of politicians—it all felt hopeless. She squeezed her daughter's hand tighter, relishing its warmth. *I won't let her grow up in a world like this.*

She breathed deeply through the mask, feeling the cool, filtered air fill her lungs. *Stay strong. For her.* Yet one question gnawed at her: How much longer? How much longer could they endure this life of constant fear? A cold shiver ran down her spine at the thought that things might still get worse.

CHAPTER 1
ROBERT BENNET –
ELLA IN THE HOSPITAL

Robert Bennet felt the oppressive silence in the room, broken only by Martha's restless breathing. She sat on the sofa, shoulders hunched, fingers digging deep into the armrest as if it were the only thing keeping her from completely breaking down.

He watched her for a while, remembering how unwavering she used to be. Martha, the woman who always used to have his back. Now, he saw only a shadow of her former self. The weight of the years, the smog, the fear for Ella—all of it had worn her down.

"I... I can't, Robert. The air... I just can't do it." Her fingers dug even deeper into the armrest, as if fearing its toxicity might pull her outside. Tears gathered in her eyes, a deep despair haunting them. "Every time I even think about leaving the apartment, my chest tightens. It's as if every breath becomes torture. Please understand."

Bennet sat down beside her and took her trembling hands in his. He recalled her doing the same, years ago when he came home utterly exhausted after a long day, having successfully completed an important project. *We've always gotten through everything together.* "Martha, please. Ella needs us. We'll manage this together. I'm here with you, okay?"

She looked at him, and for a moment, he thought he saw the fire he missed in her eyes. "Maybe... maybe I can try," she whispered, nodding hesitantly.

Slowly, she stood up; her legs felt like lead. Bennet helped her into the protective suit and carefully placed the breathing mask on her. Martha shook but clung to him as if his presence gave her the necessary strength. Together, they walked to the door, each step a small triumph. As Bennet opened the door and the cool, toxic air wafted in, something changed in Martha. Her breathing became faster and shallower, and her eyes widening in panic. "Robert, I... I can't," she stammered, frozen. "The air... it's everywhere." Her hand clutched his arm tightly, desperately trying to hold on, unable to take another step.

"Hey, hey, it's okay, Martha. Breathe. Nice and easy. You can do this. Think of Ella."

But it was too late. Martha's heart raced, sweat appeared on her forehead, and she began to hyperventilate. "I can't, Robert! I can't!" She stumbled back into the living room, her hands frantically searching for support until they found the back of the sofa.

Bennet followed her, quietly closing the door behind him. "It's okay, Martha. You don't have to." Gently, he pulled her into his arms. "I'll tell Ella that you love her and will come to her as soon as possible."

Martha clung to him, tears streaming down her cheeks. Bennet felt her despair, how she grasped at him as if he could shield her from the overwhelming emotions engulfing her. "I'm so sorry, Robert. I really wanted to try."

He held her close and gently stroked her back. "It's alright. You tried. That's what matters. We'll find a way to get through this together."

"Thank you, Robert. Thank you for understanding." Slowly, Martha released him and sat back down on the sofa, still trembling. Bennet looked at her for a moment, then nodded decisively. He needed to go to Ella now.

With a heavy heart, Bennet stepped out into the misty evening in his usual protective gear. The silence was broken only by the distant wail of a siren, the deserted streets seeming to bear the weight of his worries. The subway was almost empty. Only one other passenger sat at the end of the car. Bennet raised his hand in a brief greeting, but the man stared motionlessly ahead, intensifying Bennet's sense of isolation and loneliness.

A few days earlier, he, Martha, and Ella had taken a short walk despite the harmful air quality, and against their better judgment, hoping the protective masks would shield them from the worst effects of the smog. Shortly after their return, Ella had suffered a severe asthma attack. Her grandparents had reacted immediately, but her shortness of breath was so acute that they had to rush her to the hospital. She was diagnosed with extreme irritation of the airways due to toxic particles in the air that had penetrated even through the mask. This incident had not only hit Ella physically hard, it had also intensified her family's constant worry about her health and future. For Martha, the experience was a shock so deep that she had since refused to set even one foot outside. Bennet's decision to visit Ella in the hospital was driven by the urgent desire to offer closeness and comfort in a time marked by uncertainty and fear.

As he slipped his subway ticket back into his wallet, his gaze fell by chance on some keepsake photos. He pulled them out and examined them closely, each one telling stories of adventures and successes, but also of loneliness and distance from his family. As Bennet went through the old photos, a wave of painful memories washed over him.

He held a picture of himself in the vast oil fields of Mexico. The sun had burned his face lobster-red, and the euphoria of discovering a new oil well had been overwhelming. The next photo showed him beaming with pride on an oil rig in the North Sea, the rough waves in the background. *We thought we were heroes shaping the future. Instead, we propelled ourselves towards our own destruction.*

The feeling of invincibility they had felt during their nightly celebrations now seemed naive, oblivious to the ecological damage resulting from their work. It was only years later that Bennet fully grasped the magnitude of his actions. The thick smog layer that darkened the sky and poisoned the air was a silent witness to what he had helped cause. *What have I done?* He set the photo aside carefully.

Bennet saw himself—driven by ambition and naivety—and felt deep shame. His best years had helped usher in the Gray Winter, a catastrophe that afflicted the entire world, including his beloved granddaughter. But from this shame grew a resolve. As a former engineer in the oil industry, he knew he could now use his knowledge for something good, educating people on the dangers of environmental pollution, informing them of the importance of sustainable energy sources and actively engaging in environmental organizations.

I can't undo the past, but I can damn well try to save the future.

With this thought, he pulled out the last photo. It showed his daughter Judith holding little Ella as a baby. Once more, he realized how much Judith resembled her mother, Martha. Her facial features, the radiant smile, and the mahogany curls shimmering in the sunlight strongly reminded him of the young woman he had met many years ago on a windy day at the coast.

Martha had been sitting in a small café back then, the window wide open to the stormy sea. It was as if he were reliving it: she was reading a book about local history while the wind tousled her hair, and every time she turned a page, the sunlight caught her curls. Bennet, originally just looking for a quick coffee, had discovered himself in a conversation that ranged from everyday trivialities to profound thoughts about the country's future. The memory of that day, of Martha's lively eyes and infectious smile, brought a rare smile to his lips in the bleak environment of the subway. Martha had something fascinating about her, a unique blend of intelligence and warmth that irresistibly attracted him from the very beginning. They had spent the entire afternoon in the café, and when the sun finally set, both knew that something special would come from this chance meeting.

In the following years, they had experienced many highs and lows together. Their marriage was not always easy, especially when the environmental crisis began and Martha became increasingly plagued by anxieties, but their love and deep understanding for each other had carried them through the hardest times. As Bennet now traveled through the dark tunnels of the city, he felt a sharp pang of regret that Martha could not be by his side.

When he reached the stop for the hospital and left the subway, he still held the photo of Judith and Ella firmly in his hand. It strengthened his resolve to do everything in his power to secure a better future for Ella and all the children of her generation.

He paused briefly in front of Ella's room and looked through the door's window. A heavy lump formed in his throat as he saw her lying there, pale and fragile, the oxygen mask on her delicate face. The monitors blinked in the background. After taking a deep breath, he slowly opened the door and entered. As he approached her, a faint smile flitted across her face. "Hey, Grandpa!" Her voice was quiet, but joy flashed in her blue eyes as she saw him.

Bennet sat down beside her, gently squeezing her small hand—it felt fragile. "Hey, my brave girl. How are you?"

"I'm a bit tired," she murmured, her voice muffled by the mask. "But better, I think... Where's Grandma?"

Bennet sighed. "She... she couldn't come. She's not feeling so well, but she's thinking of you all the time and sends you all her love." He kissed her forehead and felt how much he wanted to protect her in this poisoned world.

Ella, only eight years old, had been struggling with severe asthma for years—a condition that made her particularly vulnerable. The increasingly poor air quality had further burdened her sensitive respiratory system, which explained her frequent hospital stays. Ella's asthma was so severe that she required special therapies that were not possible to perform at home.

A knock on the door announced a visitor. Dr. Simmons entered, his face serious but friendly. "Good evening, Mr. Bennet. Good evening, Ella. How are you today?"

Ella smiled weakly. "A bit better, I think."

Dr. Simmons nodded and turned to Bennet. "Could we speak outside for a moment?"

Bennet followed the doctor into the hallway; his knees felt like jelly, and all sorts of terrifying scenarios played out in his head. His heart raced, and his hands were sweaty with fear. "Dr. Simmons, how is Ella?" he asked in a trembling voice.

The doctor placed a hand on his shoulder. "She is stable but still in a critical condition. Her lungs are severely irritated by the smog. We are administering high-dose bronchodilators to widen her airways and steroids to reduce inflammation. Furthermore, she is receiving continuous oxygen to help with her breathing."

"But she's getting better, isn't she?" Bennet asked anxiously.

"We are seeing slight improvements. Her oxygen saturation has stabilized, and the inflammation in her airways is slowly decreasing, but she still requires intensive monitoring and care."

A sharp pain shot through Bennet. "Why is Ella so severely affected? There are many children with asthma, but she seems particularly susceptible."

"Ella's asthma is extreme. Her lungs are particularly susceptible to the effects of pollution, a combination of her genetic predisposition and our environmental conditions. That's why it's important to improve air quality and keep her away from triggers," explained Dr. Simmons. "Here in the hospital, we use the best air purifiers, something that has already helped her a lot."

Bennet nodded slowly, but the worry remained. "Thank you, Doctor. We'll do everything we can to protect her."

Dr. Simmons leaned forward. His voice remained warm and reassuring. "She's a strong girl, Mr. Bennet. With your support and our treatment, I'm confident she will continue to recover."

Encouraged, Bennet returned to his granddaughter, determined to give her strength and hope. "Ella, you're doing great," he said gently. "We are incredibly proud of you and will do everything to make you well again."

Ella forced a tired smile, but her eyes remained sad, as if she didn't understand why she was being praised. "Thank you, Grandpa..."

After a brief silence, her face suddenly brightened, and with the unbridled enthusiasm that only children have, she asked, "Grandpa, do you want to play cards?"

Bennet grinned and sat down next to her. "Sure thing, my little one! Let's see who wins."

Ella reached for the cards and began slowly shuffling them, her movements still a bit tired but full of concentration. "I'm going to beat you this time, Grandpa," she said with a mischievous smile as she dealt the cards.

Bennet laughed. He felt the tension leave him. "I believe you, my card queen," he joked, taking the cards. They played, and for a brief moment, the troubles of the world outside seemed to fade.

Despite the oxygen mask, Ella laughed and joked. Her joy filled the room and warmed Bennet's heart. The time spent together brought a rare, genuine smile to his face—a welcome distraction from his worries.

After several rounds, Ella looked up. "Grandpa, when are Mom and Dad coming?"

"They are working hard, princess. Your mom and dad are helping to find new ways to produce environmentally friendly energy. They are doing everything they can so that fewer children like you have to go to the hospital," Bennet explained gently.

"They make clean energy, right? So there's less smog and the air gets better," Ella asked with a hopeful look.

"Yes, exactly, my treasure. Your parents are harnessing the forces of nature. Imagine giant windmills capturing the wind, and solar panels, like big mirrors on roofs or wide fields, capturing the sun's rays. This energy then lights up our homes without creating dirty air."

A smile flitted across Ella's lips as she listened to her grandfather's words. "And this energy really doesn't make any dirt?"

"Exactly, my princess. It's like medicine for the Earth."

Ella furrowed her brow thoughtfully. "So, Mom and Dad are like doctors for the Earth?"

"Yes, you could say that. They heal the Earth, and everyone who protects the environment helps with that."

"I hope that one day I can help the Earth too," Ella said

resolutely. Her eyes sparkled.

Bennet squeezed her hand. "You will, princess. You and all the children of your generation can make our world better."

Conversations like this further strengthened their bond. Despite the stressful situation, they both found comfort and hope in their plans for the future. It was a small but significant moment of confidence in an otherwise difficult time.

At that moment, the door opened, and a friendly nurse entered. "Ella, would you like me to help you get ready for bed?" she asked with a gentle smile.

Ella yawned sleepily. "Yes, please." She set the cards aside. "Will you stay with me until I fall asleep, Grandpa?"

"Of course, princess," Bennet answered softly. He sat down beside her on a chair.

"We'll be right back." The nurse helped Ella up, and the two disappeared into the bathroom.

After a few minutes, the little girl returned, wrapped in her pajamas, and the nurse helped her put on the breathing mask. "There, everything is fine. Good night, Ella," she said before quietly leaving the room.

Ella snuggled under the blanket and turned her head to Bennet. "Goodnight, Grandpa," she whispered, her eyelids already half-closed.

"Goodnight, my princess," Bennet replied lovingly. He watched as Ella slowly fell asleep, his thoughts drifting to bittersweet memories.

In recent months, Ella had spent more time with him and Martha than at home with her parents. Judith, his daughter, was often away on business—just like he had been back then. This caused mixed feelings: joy at being able to make up for some of the time he had lost with his daughter, and pain at the fact that Judith had taken the same path he had.

As he listened to Ella's steady breathing, he realized how precious these moments were—a gift, a second chance to put his family first, having often failed to do so before. And although he was proud of Judith's work in the field of renewable energy—a critical need in a society consuming more and more energy—he wished that she would one day find a way to better balance career and family.

Bennet stayed by Ella's side until her breathing became deep and calm. He held her hand until her grip loosened and she surrendered to sleep. With a quiet sigh, he stood up, carefully tucked her in, and gently stroked her hair before quietly slipping out of the room.

The corridor was quiet and deserted, the other visitors having already left. The soft flicker of the lighting cast shadows on the walls that accompanied him on his way to the exit. His footsteps echoed lonely in the corridors, a sharp contrast to the day's hustle and bustle.

Before Bennet left the hospital, he put on the provided plastic suit and donned the breathing mask. As he stepped outside, the cool night air hit him, but soon the smog grew thicker. The toxic particles penetrated his airways despite the mask burning in his throat. He began to cough. His breathing became labored; panic overcame him. Trembling, he felt for his mask and forced himself to breathe more shallowly. In his mind's eye, he saw Ella concentrating as she shuffled the playing cards.

For Ella. He took another step forward.

Each breath burned like shards of glass in his throat. Darkness and smog merged into a hostile mass around him. *Don't give up, keep going!* He ignored the oppressive tightness in his chest and dragged himself forward despite the burning pain in his lungs.

His legs grew stiff. The image of Martha waiting for him at home strengthened his will. He could not give up. *I can do this.* He pushed on through the ghostly streets.

Finally, Bennet reached the subway station, where the purifiers were running at full capacity. Exhausted, he leaned against the wall and drew the decontaminated air deeply through the filters of his mask. The world around him appeared muted and unreal in the station's artificial lighting, but he had made it. At least for now, he had survived.

CHAPTER 2
HANNAH KOWALSKI –
THE GRAY MORNING

Dr. Hannah Kowalski looked at the environmental monitor. Red. The air was hazardous to health; she knew that immediately. She didn't need to check the risk categories—she knew them by heart. Green meant clean air, but she hadn't seen that in years. Yellow was possibly risky for particularly sensitive people, and orange harmed the weakest. But red, the ubiquitous red, meant that no one could go outside without protection. Lately, the monitor often switched to violet—the level at which the air was so toxic that, even with protective measures, everyone would struggle to breathe. *How much longer until Level Maroon is reached?* This, the highest danger level, meant that no life would remain. *That must never happen—I will prevent it.*

Before leaving the apartment, Hannah looked at herself in the mirror. A slender woman in her thirties, with serious eyes and fine lines around her mouth—traces of worry and tension that had especially defined her daily life as an environmental scientist since the onset of the Gray Winter—stared back at her. Her once radiant, healthy skin appeared tired and pale. She brushed a limp strand of dark blonde hair from her face.

Looking like this, I certainly won't be winning any beauty contests. She twisted her mouth into a wry smile, there were much more important things to worry about right now. Her mission was to stop the Gray Winter.

With a deep sigh, she expertly donned her breathing mask and then pulled on a thin plastic suit. Combined with a protective hood, gloves, and goggles, she was as shielded as possible from the ubiquitous dirt particles outside. One last scrutinizing look in the mirror. *Oh, looks almost better than before.* She involuntarily began to laugh—a bright, liberating sound that dissolved the oppressive atmosphere for a moment.

Suddenly, her mobile phone vibrated in her pocket, and she laboriously pulled it out from under the protective suit. The display showed a message from her mother:

Dad had trouble breathing again last night. I'm worried.

A queasy feeling spread through Hannah, and she immediately pressed call.

"Mom? It's me, Hannah. What happened? How is Dad?"

"Oh, Hannah, it's so good to hear your voice." Her mother sounded exhausted, and there was something else in her tone, as if she had been crying all night. "It was terrible. Your father could hardly breathe. We had to call the emergency doctor."

Hannah felt her heart clench painfully, but she forced herself to remain calm so as not to alarm her mother. "How is he now?" she asked, suppressing her growing concern with a deep breath.

"He's resting, but the doctors say he's very weak," her mother replied, her voice trembling. "They were able to help him, but they don't know how much longer he can hold on, and they even advised that he wear a mask indoors to reduce exposure to the toxic air."

"This damn air pollution!" Hannah burst out. "I'm so sorry I can't be there with you."

"I know, dear," her mother said tiredly. "We're going to stay inside now and have everything we need delivered. Even here in the countryside, the air is getting worse. The air purifiers just can't keep up anymore. It's getting worse and worse." Her voice quavered, then she broke into tears. "I'm so afraid he won't make it."

"That won't happen," Hannah said, realizing she was trying to convince herself as well, and failing. Fear crept up inside her. "Mom, listen, I'll ask at the institute for the best air filters. Maybe new ones have been developed. I'll make sure you get them."

"Oh, Hannah, that would be wonderful," her mother whispered gratefully. "But, darling, how are things with you? Are you remembering to take your medication regularly?"

Hannah took a deep breath. "Yes, Mom, I don't forget them." She wanted to reassure her mother and change the subject. "Finally, the special biofilms for air purification are fully developed. You know how long we've been working on them. They're made from microorganisms like bacteria and algae, specifically trained to filter and break down pollutants in the air. When implemented, they should significantly improve air quality."

"That sounds incredible. Do you think it will really help?"

"Yes, Mom, I'm sure," Hannah said with a small smile. "These biofilms are much more efficient than anything we've had before. They filter and neutralize pollutants directly from the air. If we deploy them in cities, or even in the countryside, they can clean the air effectively and save many lives."

"Hannah, that would truly be a blessing. We so desperately need a solution."

"Mom, I'm doing what I can, I promise," Hannah said, making every effort to suppress her uncertainty. Her mother had always been the strong one—the woman who comforted her when she was plagued by nightmares as a child. Now it was up to her to be strong. "We'll find a way, okay? I won't let you down." She fought against the feeling of helplessness rising within her. "Be brave. We'll get through this together."

"I know, dear," came the quiet reply, laced with a weakness that Hannah could hardly bear. *What has happened to the woman who always had everything under control, who was our rock?*

"Take care of yourself, sweetheart. We love you." With these words, her mother said goodbye.

"I love you too," said Hannah. She hung up and let the

mobile phone drop. Her hands were damp. She wanted to take a deep breath, but the mask suddenly felt suffocating. With a swift movement, she tore it off. Leaning against the cold wall of her hallway, a feeling of helplessness overcame her. Her father was in danger. She shook her head and wiped away a tear. Now was not the time to be weak. She had to act.

Hannah turned around and looked at her small but cozy apartment. The walls were lined with tall shelves densely packed with specialized literature on environmental science and climate change, interspersed with classics and thrilling adventure novels. These books, which she had voraciously devoured before the Gray Winter, reflected her curiosity and her desire to understand the world she now wanted to save. Her gaze lingered on the small indoor garden she had once created with so much love. Plants like aloe vera, small succulents, and a delicate ficus grew there. She noticed the wilted leaves and dry soil with a sense of melancholy—a silent reproach resulting from her lack of attention. Her professional obligations—the endless analysis of environmental data and communication with international colleagues—consumed almost every waking minute of her days.

Next to the books, Hannah spotted a small fossil that stood on a shelf. It was a special find from her childhood. She vividly remembered the day she had found the fossilized imprint of a long-extinct plant in a piece of stone, and her father had sat down with her to patiently explain how this imprint had formed over millions of years. "This is a window into the past," he had said enthusiastically. "It shows us what life looked like unimaginably long ago."

She remembered the days by the river. Together, she and her father had watched frogs and dragonflies. The fascination and awe she had felt back then was still present. "When I grow up, I want to be a biologist," had been her conviction at the time. These moments had ignited in Hannah a deep love for nature and awakened in her the desire to protect the environment. And indeed, years later, she had begun studying biology. She would have finished the course, too, if it hadn't been for a seminar by Professor John Weber that changed everything. His passionate lectures about the escalating environmental crisis and his visionary solutions made her realize that she wanted more than just to research—she wanted to act. So, she switched to environmental sciences, determined to contribute to saving nature.

With a final glance at the red-glowing environmental monitor, she stepped out of the apartment. Today was one of those days when she had to muster all her strength to make it to work. The heavy backpack—in it a laptop, along with the notes and sketches she had made during sleepless nights—pulled at her shoulders.

The silence in the hallway was so dense that Hannah could hear both her own footsteps and the soft suction of her breathing through the mask. Every time she passed an apartment door, she heard the familiar hum of air purifiers inside. Each of her steps rebounded, amplifying the feeling of isolation. In the lobby, she encountered the janitor, Mr. Schmidt, who was mopping the floor. He gave her a tired smile. "Good morning, Doctor. It's looking bad out there," he remarked, his tone muted.

"Yes, unfortunately. Stay indoors, Mr. Schmidt. It's safer," she replied as she opened the main door. Gray morning air struck her; the smog was so dense that even the outlines of the buildings vanished in the haze. Her eyes burned despite the protective goggles she wore. Every breath was a challenge, even through the mask.

On the way to the subway station, Hannah encountered hardly a soul. The city lay still and abandoned under the thick smog. As she turned the corner, her gaze lingered on a familiar silhouette. "Mikael?" she called out, her voice an uncertain echo in the empty street.

Mikael turned around. Through the dense fog, she could make out his athletic build and his dark curls peeking out from under the protective hood. His eyes looked thoughtful and worried, but when he recognized her, they brightened—a gentle glow in the bleak surroundings.

"Hannah," he exclaimed happily. "What a surprise to see you here!"

They met during their university days and had worked on

many projects together, but lost touch after graduation.

Hannah's heart skipped a beat. "I haven't seen you in ages," she replied, her voice muffled by the breathing mask. In this inhospitable environment, where silence usually prevailed, his presence was very welcome.

Mikael nodded solemnly. "Yes, unfortunately the circumstances aren't the best for a reunion. How are you? I heard you're working at the institute, exploring solutions for all of this." He gestured helplessly into the fog.

Hannah sighed heavily and walked cautiously beside him. "I'm doing my best, Mikael, but sometimes it just feels overwhelming. How are things with you? I've seen you're quite active on social media and tirelessly advocating for environmental protection."

Mikael's face darkened. "It's damn hard, Hannah. We're trying to force the government to do more, but they're just reacting too slowly. Their measures are simply ridiculous." He shook his head in frustration.

Hannah nodded vigorously. "I know exactly what you mean. Sometimes it feels so hopeless, but we mustn't give up." She paused briefly and added quietly, "Rumor has it that a new air filtration technology will soon be deployed that could change everything."

Mikael shook his head. "I don't know, Hannah... These miracle solutions... How often have they disappointed us? What if—"

"What if it's different this time?" Hannah said, interrupting him. "It's true, there's still a lot we need to find out. We're also working on a project on biofilms that is almost finished, and I'm placing great hopes on it. What if these technologies actually work? We have to seize every chance we have left."

As they spoke, they approached the next subway station. Despite the heavy air and the oppressive atmosphere created by the smog, Hannah felt somewhat lighter in Mikael's presence. It was a small reminder that she wasn't fighting the environmental crisis alone.

"Hannah, I'm actually on my way to the hospital," Mikael said, his voice even more serious and sadder than before. "Mr.

Sutter, my neighbor, is there because of his chronic bronchitis. His condition has dramatically worsened in the last few days. The doctors aren't very optimistic. We've spent a lot of time together in recent months. He's alone, like me, something that brought us together."

Hannah's heart tightened at his words. She thought of her own father and his frail health. She placed her gloved hand on Mikael's arm—a gesture of comfort, even if the touch was muted through the protective gear. "I'm so sorry," she said quietly. "If there's anything I can do, please let me know."

Mikael took a deep breath, his voice trembling with despair. "How can we end this nightmare? Living in this toxic air every day is unbearable. And it's getting worse. What happens if we can't breathe at all in a few months?"

Hannah felt the weight of Mikael's question pressing on her heart. His worries mirrored her own, but she remained calm and resolute. "Mikael, I know it's hard, but I promise you, I will do everything to defeat the Gray Winter. Scientists all over the world are working tirelessly, day and night." She paused, her voice becoming gentler yet firm. "We'll make it. Please don't lose hope."

"Thank you, Hannah. It's good to know that you're not giving up. That gives me some hope." As they reached the subway station, they embraced to say goodbye—a moment of connection amid the bleak reality.

Just then, her phone vibrated again, and she hastily pulled it out. On the display, a message from Simon Carson, a member of her team, lit up. Her heart skipped a beat as she read it.

Urgent: Hannah, there was an incident with the new bioreactor. Our research is in danger! We need you at the institute immediately. Please come quickly. Where are you?

Panic rose in her throat; her thoughts raced. An incident with a bioreactor... This can't happen, not now! The bioreactors housed the sensitive biofilms she had worked on for years. If they were destroyed, everything would be lost. All the work that could potentially reverse decades of environmental damage would be wiped out within hours.

"I have to go, Mikael," she pressed out in a choked voice, already rushing toward the next train. Behind her, she could still hear his concerned voice wishing her well. She nodded hastily without turning around.

CHAPTER 3
HANNAH KOWALSKI –
WARNING SIGNS

After a short but tense ride, Hannah reached the state research institute. The building stood like an unshakable fortress amid the smog-covered city, its facades equipped with special air filtration systems and its entrances hermetically sealed to prevent the toxic outside air from entering. It demonstrated its pioneering role in the fight against environmental pollution and symbolized hope for a better, cleaner future.

Hannah swiped her access card through the reader and entered the airlock. As she carefully removed her protective clothing and placed it into containers designated for cleaning and reuse, the storm of worries in her head seemed to rage ever more fiercely. Her research—years of work—was in danger. She stepped into the air shower, but the jets didn't immediately commence like usual. For a moment, she felt as if time stood still. Her hands tingled slightly. Unconsciously, she massaged her fingers. Her thoughts raced: *What if everything is lost? What if we have to start all over again?* Finally, the air shower blew strong gusts, whirling dust and particles from her clothing. Only then did the second door of the airlock open, and she entered the interior.

Her gaze immediately fell on Simon Carson, who seemed to have been waiting for her. His reddish-blond hair stood wildly, as if he had nervously run his hands through it multiple times. With his distinctive but unobtrusive facial features, he might not have been a heartthrob, but it was his charismatic smile that instantly made him likable. The green eyes, which usually shone warmly and vividly, were now clouded with worry. He paced nervously in the corridor, clutching a tablet tightly to his chest.

"Hannah, we have a serious problem in Sector C. The new bioreactor overheated overnight. This morning, the temperature was over 50 degrees Celsius. The cooling system seems to have failed," said Simon, showing her the current data on his tablet.

Hannah felt her heartbeat accelerate, but she forced herself to remain calm. "What about the biofilms?"

"I immediately transferred them to one of the older reactors that's connected to the automatic monitoring system," Simon replied.

"Well done." Hannah pulled out her phone. "We need to act quickly and find out how extensive the damage is." She hastily dialed a number. "Elise? Could you please come right away with Robert and Laura to the conference room next to the lab?"

Shortly thereafter, the team gathered around a large table. Hannah looked into the tense faces of her colleagues.

"First, we need to determine if the biofilms are still alive and active," she began. "What tests would be most appropriate for that?"

Dr. Elise Mertens, the microbiologist, was the first to speak up. "We could begin with a microscopic examination. If I look at the cells under the microscope, I can determine if they're still intact."

"That would be a good start," agreed Dr. Robert Meier as he reviewed his notes. "But it would also be important to conduct enzyme activity tests. If the enzymes in the biofilms are still active, we'll know the microorganisms are still alive."

"Sounds reasonable. What do you think, Laura?"

Dr. Laura Fischer, who had been silently listening to the discussion so far, nodded slightly. "I think a DNA analysis would also be helpful. That way, we can ensure that the composition of the biofilms has remained stable. But I suggest we perform the microscopic and enzymatic tests first and then use the DNA analysis as a supplement."

Hannah considered this proposal briefly. "Good, that sounds like a sensible plan. Elise and Robert, please report back as soon as you have the results. Laura, be ready for the DNA analysis. We need results quickly."

The team got straight to work, taking the necessary samples and disappearing into their respective labs.

Hannah went to her office and sank heavily into her chair, the old leather creaking softly under her weight. She closed her eyes for a moment, having done everything within her power. The biofilms were now safe—there was nothing left for her to do but to wait for the test results. She knew exactly that the stress wasn't good for her. With slow, deliberate breaths, she tried to dissolve her inner restlessness and actively calm her pulse—a technique her physiotherapist had shown her. Mechanically, she reached for her cup of tea, which, as always, stood ready on her desk. The ceramic mug felt cool to the touch. As she took the first sip, an unpleasant shiver ran through her—the tea was cold and bitter. "Of course..." she murmured, shaking her head, her voice full of resignation. With a sigh, she stood up and went to the kitchen to brew herself a fresh cup. Such small rituals gave her a sense of normalcy in a world that was increasingly falling apart.

Back in the office, her gaze was inevitably drawn to an old, visibly worn photograph pinned to the bulletin board behind her monitor. The picture showed her and Professor Weber smiling in front of a poster of their joint research at a conference in Vienna. They had won their first prize there. The photo, a silent testimony of times past, evoked a flood of memories.

Hannah took the picture from the bulletin board and looked at it with a wistful smile. When she turned it over, her eyes fell on Professor Weber's handwritten message:

Your research will change the world, Hannah. I'm proud that you're part of our team.

These words had meant so much to her back then—and even

today, they still moved her.

Her chest filled with a mixture of pride and sadness. Professor Weber's belief in her and her mission had become an unwavering anchor in her life, supporting her, especially on days marked by deep despair and hopelessness.

Weber's unexpected death—ironically caused by the air pollution he had fought against all his life—left a deep void in Hannah's life, but also drove her to step into his shoes and continue his legacy with even greater commitment. Today, as the leader of a research team, she faced the same challenge that Weber had once confronted: analyzing current data while finding new ways to minimize environmental impacts.

Her thoughts wandered to her father. The worry about him weighed heavily on her heart. Added to that were the problems with the biofilms. *How much longer can this go on?* Once again, she tried to focus on her work. It felt like she was fighting a never-ending battle. Determined, she entered the control room, a relic of Professor Weber's efforts. In front of her, screens flickered with the latest data from the air quality monitoring stations in Plainfield. Hannah's eyes narrowed as she scrutinized the numbers and graphs. At first glance, it was clear that some of the curves had shot up alarmingly. The values for particulate matter and nitrogen oxides had reached dizzying levels, far beyond the internationally accepted limits. She blinked several times to make sure the numbers were real. Air pollution was rapidly increasing, and immediate action was unavoidable.

One graph stood out among all the others: the particulate matter levels in the city center had exceeded 150 micrograms per cubic meter—a threatening number, far above the safe limits stated in the international health guidelines. Hannah's pulse quickened as her eyes glided along the red bars. These values were not just worrying, they were catastrophic. At the same time, the nitrogen oxide levels showed a dramatic increase. They were almost twice as high as the permitted limits. In recent days, the environmental monitor had already switched to violet multiple times, indicating that such extreme conditions were now occurring more frequently.

The numbers screamed for immediate action. Hannah reached for the phone and dialed the number of Dr. Harold Vogel, the institute's director. A monotonous, busy signal droned in the receiver. With a snort, she finally hung up, annoyed.

Determined, she pulled her laptop closer to record her thoughts in an email, but as her fingers touched the keys, they felt strangely numb; her hands were tingling again. She suppressed the rising panic and forced herself to stay calm. *Not now. I have to function.*

The ringing of the telephone tore her from her thoughts. She hastily grabbed the receiver, relieved by the interruption. "Hannah, this is Dr. Vogel. You wanted to speak with me?"

In a composed voice, she described her observations of the alarming air quality data, then proceeded to propose measures. "We should form a task force focused on reducing pollutant emissions and developing radical solutions. Also, a report with the current data and analyses must be sent to the Ministry of the Environment as soon as possible to make the situation visible at the highest level and to prompt quick responses on a political level."

"Those sound like sensible proposals," Dr. Vogel agreed. "I'll make sure the authorities finally step on the gas."

A wave of relief flooded over Hannah. "Thank you, Dr. Vogel. It's important that we act immediately."

"I understand. Please continue to work out your proposals. I'll take the necessary steps."

After hanging up, she cast a quick glance at her inbox, but the results of the microscopy and enzyme tests had not yet arrived.

In the next few hours, Hannah worked intently, turning her ideas into concrete actions—plans for stricter emission regulations and the introduction of urban green spaces. Her thoughts drifted to the smog towers she knew had been implemented in Asia. She sketched how such systems could also help in Plainfield. Time and again, she glanced at the clock, hoping the test results would soon arrive.

Finally, her computer beeped. The results were in. Her heart raced as she opened the file and began to read.

Elise had completed the microscopic examinations.

Hannah, the biofilms are severely damaged. Under the microscope, I see that most of the cells are destroyed. Only a few particularly resistant bacteria and fungi have survived. The protozoa and algae are completely dead. The heat of over 50°C has killed almost everything.

Hannah felt her stomach knot. Her vision blurred, but she forced herself to keep going, opening Robert's enzyme test results.

Hannah, the enzyme activity has almost completely ceased. Those still active can no longer effectively break down the pollutants. It appears the biofilms have lost their function.

Hannah closed her eyes and rested her head in her hands, her elbows firmly planted on the table. A dull roaring filled her ears. She felt tears welling up. Her mind drifted to early mornings when the world was still asleep and only the soft hum of the lab equipment kept her company. She thought of the late nights with cold coffee and eyes nearly closing from exhaustion—struggling to stay awake to analyze yet another refinement of the biofilm, eager to see if it may prove more effective in eliminating pollutants. Step by step, progress had been made, and they finally developed the perfect biofilm. But now... everything was destroyed. The realization hit her like a truck, and for a moment, she felt overwhelmed by the futility of her work.

A knock pulled her from her thoughts. She lifted her head and saw Simon Carson standing in the doorway.

"Hannah, I just wanted to say goodbye," he began uncertainly. "As you know, I'll be at InnoTech for some time, starting tomorrow. It's about the final touches for the new air filtration technology. I hope I can make a valuable contribution there."

Feeling a lump in her throat, Hannah swallowed hard. Simon leaving hurt more than she had expected. "Yes, of course, I remember," she said, striving to keep her voice steady. "That's important, especially now that our project lies in ruins..."

Simon took a step closer, and she could perceive the familiar scent of his aftershave. His eyes searched hers, as if wanting to say something, but the words remained unspoken. For a moment, the world seemed to stand still. Hannah's heart beat faster, and she felt a warmth spreading in her chest.

His gaze drifted to her lips and then back to her eyes. It felt as if everything depended on this one moment. But then Simon lowered his head, uncertainty reflected in his features. "What will you do now?"

Hannah looked away and tucked a strand of hair behind her ear. "I'll thaw the frozen biofilm samples. They weren't optimal when we preserved them, but it's a start. It will take months to cultivate them again and bring them to the desired level—if we can even manage it again." Her voice trembled slightly. She had to fight to hold back the rising tears.

A part of her wanted to ask him to stay, to tell him how much she needed him—not just in the lab, but personally. But she knew that would be unreasonable and selfish.

Simon gently placed his hand on her shoulder, his eyes roaming over her face. The warmth of his touch sent a tingling sensation through her body. "I can cancel. It's not the right time to leave the institute..."

Hannah looked at him; their eyes met. For a heartbeat, she considered it. Then she shook her head slightly. "No, Simon. You have to go. We're counting on Clara Zheng's technology now. The Gray Winter must end."

He hesitated, his voice barely more than a whisper. "Are you sure?"

She forced a faint smile. "Absolutely sure. Besides... who knows, maybe you'll save us all with this new technology." She tried to adopt a joking tone, but her voice betrayed her.

Simon nodded slowly. "Alright," he finally said. "If you need anything—anything at all—call me."

"I will," she promised. "Take care of yourself."

He let his hand slide from her shoulder; the sudden coolness made her shiver. "See you soon, Hannah," he said softly before turning to leave.

"See you soon," she whispered as the door closed behind him.

Hannah stood for a moment, staring at the closed door. The silence in the room was overwhelming. She felt empty, drained.

The prospect of having to start all over again was devastating. And the void left by Simon's absence only amplified this feeling. When she finally moved, she noticed her hands were shaking. The tingling she had previously ignored spread through her arms. Her fingers felt numb. She massaged her hands, but it didn't help. At last, tears streamed down her cheeks.

CHAPTER 4
TV REPORT –
PAST MISTAKES

Hannah sat alone in her dimly lit living room, illuminated only by the gentle glow of the television. To save electricity, she had turned off the lights. The screen cast ghostly shadows on the walls, making the gloom that had hung over Plainfield for years feel even more oppressive. That evening, a much-publicized documentary was airing about the historical missteps that had led to the Gray Winter.

It began with footage of the Amazon rainforest—more precisely, its sorrowful remnants. Where once dense, lush jungle had stood, now stretched a barren landscape used for agricultural monocultures. Dr. Pereira, a respected environmental scientist, appeared on the screen. "Do you see this? This was once the largest rainforest in the world—the heart of our global biodiversity and the lungs of the Earth. These forests were of immeasurable ecological value."

In the background, archival footage showed heavy logging machinery tearing through the once-mighty forest. "The destruction of the Amazon has severely disrupted the global carbon dioxide balance. These forests played a key role in carbon sequestration and were among the world's largest natural carbon sinks. With their deforestation, we have lost an immense capacity to bind carbon dioxide, which has further accelerated climate change." An image showed an orphaned jaguar cub, desperately wandering the desolate landscape in search of its mother, who had fallen victim to the bulldozers. "The deforestation, in combination with the burning of biomass and fossil fuels, has not only significantly worsened air quality but has also increased the concentration of ground-level ozone, with severe health consequences for humans and animals."

The images of the orphaned jaguar cub touched Hannah deeply. She felt the pain of the creature that had lost everything and thought of the destruction plaguing Plainfield. Every day, Hannah witnessed the effects of human greed, and she had been fighting tirelessly to prevent nature from suffering further.

The documentary shifted to overcrowded streets in metropolises like Shanghai and Delhi, bursting at the seams. An elderly lady from Los Angeles reminisced wistfully, "You used to be able to walk or take the bus, but then city planning focused on private cars. Suddenly, everyone wanted automobiles. A lot of money was spent on roads and parking lots, and public transportation died off. Since air pollution escalated and we can no longer use cars, we're stuck. The cars are gone, but the smog remains..." The camera showed children in heavily polluted neighborhoods having to play indoors while toxic fog lingered outside. "My grandchildren don't know outdoor games anymore. Our parks are empty because the air is just too bad. We're afraid to let them go outside."

Hannah's mind drifted back to her own childhood. She remembered sunny days in the park—the laughter and the feeling of boundless freedom. The thought that future generations would no longer experience these simple joys filled her with a painful sense of helplessness.

A spokeswoman then appeared on screen. "These two disasters—climate change and air pollution—are inseparably connected. While climate change exacerbates weather extremes through global warming, air pollution increases the burden on the environment and human health. The smog resulting from the burning of fossil fuels amplifies global warming and simultaneously alters air currents. This leads to persistent heat that keeps pollutants in the atmosphere longer. This interplay drives us further into a vicious cycle from which escape becomes increasingly difficult.

"Environmental destruction not only brought us to this point, the way we meet our energy needs also contributed. The global phase-out of nuclear energy over the past 25 years and the increasing digitalization led to an energy crisis that delayed the transition to sustainable mobility."

An analyst appeared on the screen. "Green energy sources like solar and wind power couldn't meet the suddenly massively increased energy demand. Especially in cities where power generation through solar energy became practically impossible due to increasing smog, old coal-fired power plants were restarted—a fatal move. The priority was to supply households and digital infrastructure, which significantly delayed the implementation of plans to fully switch transportation to electric vehicles.

"The switch to electric vehicles could have made a vital contribution to reducing emissions, but due to power shortages, this transformation stalled. This led to a further worsening of air pollution in cities, as internal combustion engines remained the norm."

It's a vicious circle. Hannah bit her lip. With the air quality forcing people to spend more and more time indoors, the demand for electricity had exploded in recent years. Coal was too dirty, nuclear power too dangerous, and renewable energies were far from sufficient. With the smog blocking the sunlight, solar panels generated hardly any electricity. *We're trapped. Every step we take only worsens the situation.* Air pollution continued to increase, while dependence on fossil fuels persisted. The cycle couldn't be broken. *How much longer? How long until everything collapses?*

"The rapid growth brought economic advantages, but the price was high," explained an economic analyst. "Rapid industrialization often led to the neglect of environmental standards and to the excessive exploitation of natural resources." Images from Southeast Asia showed the devastating consequences, such as severe air and water pollution.

Dr. Linda Choi, an environmental health physician, expressed concern: "We are now seeing the dark side of unchecked industrial growth. Among other things, we have the highest rates of respiratory diseases worldwide. This alarming state is a direct consequence of our environmentally harmful practices."

Hannah thought of her brother, who lived overseas. He had reported similar conditions. Their conversations often revolved around the disturbing question of how these environmental crises would develop in the future.

"The Gray Winter has practically brought international trade to a standstill," the previous spokeswoman continued. "Each country is now fighting for its own survival, yet there is a glimmer of hope amid this global isolation. In the area of knowledge transfer and environmental technologies, international cooperation is still functioning relatively well. Particularly noteworthy is the collaboration with InnoTech, a leading technology company here in Plainfield, which is at the forefront in the fight against the climate catastrophe."

The documentary returned to the studio, back to its original presenter. Despite her petite figure, Maria Cruz impressed with her confident and professional demeanor. Her long, dark brown hair was tied in a ponytail, revealing a face with expressive dark eyes and red-painted lips. A well-known local reporter, her determined gaze and clear voice immediately captivated the audience. She never hesitated to call out problems directly and had built a reputation by persistently exposing and publicly addressing government failures.

"The term Gray Winter aptly describes the suffocating blanket of smog enveloping our cities like an eternal veil, devouring the sun. It is not just a climatic phenomenon, it also represents the growing hopelessness in our society. When people look out of their windows and see only a bleak, polluted world, they lose faith in a better future. It is a constant reminder of the wrong decisions and inaction that have brought us to this point.

She then addressed the topic of environmental monitoring. "We all know the environmental monitor, a device that seems inconspicuous at first glance, like an old thermometer, but in truth fulfills a very critical function. It continuously measures the oxygen content and the concentration of toxins in the air, summarizing the results in a risk score. Six months ago, the environmental monitors predominantly showed orange and sometimes red—warning signals for a serious health risk in Plainfield. But in recent weeks, we have observed an alarming increase in violet readings—a clear indication of extremely harmful air quality and also that the Gray Winter is worsening."

The camera zoomed closer to her face as Maria Cruz continued urgently: "When the air quality reaches the highest and most dangerous level, maroon, the situation becomes life-threatening for everyone. Then no one may leave the house—under any circumstances! Exposure to this air leads to immediate severe health emergencies like acute respiratory distress and other life-threatening conditions."

Hannah felt a shiver run through her body. *This must be prevented at all costs!*

Maria Cruz now spoke in a subdued voice, but her words struck with undiminished sharpness: "What we are experiencing today is the result of decades of political failure, uncontrolled industrialization, and the misuse of fossil fuels. This disastrous combination has not only destroyed our environment but also conjured the smog that is suffocating our cities and plunging our climate into chaos. The Gray Winter we live in today is the bitter consequence of many wrong decisions. Now we stand at a crossroads: Do we finally act, or do we watch as our world goes down in the fog of these mistakes?" Under Maria Cruz, a phone number appeared. "I would like to address another important point: The people in Plainfield are not only trapped by the toxic air—many are also struggling with oppressive loneliness. It is especially hard for singles and the elderly, who often go for days without direct contact with others. In recent months, we have received an increasing number of calls from desperate citizens. For this reason, a counseling hotline has now been set up, which you can see displayed below."

The broadcast switched to Dr. Elisabeth Kraft, who was sitting in her office. "In times of isolation and social distancing, it is crucial to find ways to maintain emotional connections," she explained. "The lack of physical contact not only affects the elderly. Younger people miss the natural interaction with friends and classmates. The older generations understand what they are missing. Children, on the other hand, are growing up in this isolation and often know only their immediate family personally. The long-term effects on their social and emotional development are difficult to estimate but could be profound.

"Our social structure is facing drastic changes. The lack of personal contact will influence how these children form future relationships and engage in society. This could fundamentally alter social dynamics."

Maria Cruz appeared on screen again. "It remains unclear where the journey we're on with the Gray Winter is leading us. But we must already think about the consequences and look for solutions that emotionally strengthen our children and adolescents especially. Don't hesitate to call the number displayed below—we are here for you." With that, the documentary ended.

Hannah's gaze remained on the dark screen, but her thoughts were elsewhere. The documentary had only strengthened her conviction: she had to continue working on the biofilms; there was no doubt about that. The images of destroyed forests and orphaned animals had reminded her of how significant her research was.

Dr. Kraft's words still echoed in her ears. *What if this isolation changes society forever?* The more she thought about it, the more she realized how much this also applied to herself. *When was the last time I met friends who weren't colleagues from the institute? When was the last time I had a conversation that wasn't about the Gray Winter?*

In recent months, her world had become ever smaller. Her life revolved only around research and the desperate hope of being able to change something. Apart from occasional phone calls with her parents, there were hardly any personal contacts. It felt as if she were just as isolated as any of the children Dr. Kraft had spoken about. Perhaps she was not only fighting the pollution out there but also the growing emptiness in her own life.

This realization hit her hard. The world outside seemed to be falling apart, but perhaps it was her own world that was dissolving first.

She reached for her mobile phone to write a message to her mother, but her fingers did not obey her. The phone slipped from her hands and fell clattering to the floor. Panic rose within her as she laboriously picked it up again. She needed help. Her attempt to dial the number failed. Finally, in a trembling voice, she commanded, "Call Dr. Kramer." The dial tone sounded, and after several endlessly long seconds, a familiar voice answered.

"Kramer speaking."

Hannah swallowed hard before whispering, "Dr. Kramer, this is Hannah Kowalski. My MS is back..."

CHAPTER 5
MIKAEL VASILAKIS –
THE VOICE OF DESPAIR

Mikael has been similarly affected by the images in the documentary. "I can't just stand by and allow this to happen," he murmured, clenching his fists. A glance out the window into the omnipresent toxic fog reinforced his determination to take to the streets today.

In his modestly furnished room, whose walls were adorned with posters from environmental organizations and past demonstrations, Mikael checked his equipment. He grabbed his old, reliable megaphone, which had served him well at many protests. After a quick battery check, he tested it briefly to ensure he would be heard among the crowd. *Today, I will raise my voice— not just for myself, but for all who suffer under the dirty air.* His expression was already combative, ready for the upcoming protest. Energetically, he put on his breathing mask, long since more than just protection against the toxins in the air. It had become a symbol of his fight—a reminder that action was needed.

Mikael Vasilakis had grown up in a small coastal town in Greece, where the sea and the stories of old fishermen had shaped his life. Influenced by these experiences, his awareness of the importance of living in harmony with nature was sharpened. Even as a child, he could listen for hours to the sound of the waves gently crashing against the cliffs and to the old fishermen recounting a time when the sea was still alive and untouched. These memories remained a painful echo that drove him.

Although Mikael passionately devoted himself to activism, the pressure from his family weighed heavily on him. "You're wasting your life," his father's voice echoed through the receiver each time Mikael talked about his projects again. Yet whenever he envisioned the devastated coasts of his homeland, he knew that he was doing the right thing.

When he first stepped onto the university campus in Plainfield years ago, for the first time, he had felt part of something bigger. There, he quickly found like-minded people with whom he organized campaigns, wrote petitions, and planned protests. Despite the sense of solidarity he experienced, his parents' words often echoed in his head. His mother's plea was always present: "Mikael, we want you to come home." The conflict between his family's expectations and his inner urge to change the world was a constant companion.

Now, holding the hand-painted banner—*For a World Without Smog* written in bold green letters—he pushed aside his doubts. As he rolled it up and grabbed the megaphone, he knew: Here, at the forefront in the fight against the Gray Winter, was where he belonged.

The sun had just risen on the horizon, but the city was already shrouded in its usual thick gray veil. The streets were, as always, deserted as Mikael set off on foot toward the government building. He had announced the action in advance on his website and had received an impressive amount of approval and support there; he expected thousands of participants.

When Mikael reached the government square and found only about 50 protesters, his first reaction was disappointment. But upon closer inspection, he recognized in each individual the same determination and courage that drove him. He understood that fear of polluted air and the associated risks of being outside had prevented many potential supporters from attending.

Mikael climbed onto a small, improvised platform and grabbed the megaphone. "My friends, we are here to fight for our right to clean air and to secure the future of our children, our families, and our city. We have seen the reports, heard the warnings, and experienced the consequences. Concern alone is not enough. It's time to act!"

Applause broke out, interrupted by energetic shouts and the waving of placards bearing slogans like *Clean Air Is Our Right!* and *Action, Not Words!* Another demonstrator carried a sign that read *Stop the Leonard Effect!*

Fueled by the reaction, Mikael raised his voice as he addressed the government: "We are also here to protest against the short-sighted political decisions that endanger our future. The Leonard Effect is a symbol of our government's failure to make the necessary bold decisions. Every day of hesitation costs innocent lives. Our children suffer, and our elderly fight for every breath. We need clear, decisive steps to reduce emissions and clean our air. We demand real solutions, not empty promises that evaporate!"

The mood among the protesters intensified; together, they loudly shouted: "We want clean air!" Their voices merged into an impressive chorus of protest. Mikael let his gaze wander over the crowd. In the faces, he saw not only anger but also hope.

"We stand here together because we believe that change is possible. Each of us has a voice, and together these voices form a cry that no one can ignore. Today, we are sending a clear message: We are awake, we are present, and we will not rest until our air is clean again!"

Mikael and the determined group waved their banners in front of the imposing government building, but no response was offered from inside to the urgent calls for action and change. The massive doors of the building remained relentlessly closed, as though shielding its occupants both physically and symbolically from the people's demands.

A TV crew emerged from the fog and headed directly toward Mikael and his fellow activists. Maria Cruz, pointed her microphone at Mikael while the cameraman captured the scene. "Could you please briefly introduce yourself to our viewers and explain why you're here today?" Maria had to almost shout to be heard over the loud chanting of the crowd in the background.

Mikael felt the significance of the moment as he spoke into the camera. "I am Mikael Vasilakis, environmental activist. Our government must act now! Every breath we take in this polluted air brings us closer to the brink. Waiting is no longer an option!" he shouted, his voice filled with burning passion. He thrust his fist skywards in a clear symbol of resistance. Promptly, the protesters responded with a tremendous echo of approval that vibrated through the air. Their shouts and thunderous applause formed a powerful wave of solidarity that added even more weight to Mikael's words.

Some of the demonstrators stepped in front of the camera to share their personal stories. An elderly woman, whose eyes reflected the depth of her suffering, spoke about the breathing difficulties she and her husband had to endure daily. Next to her, a young student took the floor. "It's not only the government's task to research and implement innovative air purification solutions. Each of us must be part of the solution. We need to change our thinking and actions to overcome this crisis. Every contribution counts. We are here because we don't want to leave our future to the forces of inertia and hesitation," he explained with a clear, firm voice, making his words resonate profoundly.

The reporter nodded her understanding and turned back to the camera. "As you can see, the situation here is extremely serious. These people's determination to be heard is unmistakable. Air pollution is not an abstract statistic, it has a profound impact on the daily lives of the entire city's population, and its reach stretches far beyond." With these words, she ended the recording, and the TV crew departed as quickly into the fog as they had appeared.

"That was important," Mikael murmured to one of his fellow activists. "Every camera, every interview helps us spread our message further. We need the public on our side to increase the pressure on the government." The others nodded in agreement, and Mikael felt the affirmation that their protest was being heard beyond this square.

Suddenly, a group of uniformed security forces pushed through the crowd, led by a tall man whose expensive suit was clearly visible under the transparent plastic protection. The demonstrators stepped back, intimidated.

The man in the suit approached the platform and waved the security forces back. "Who's in charge here?" His assertive demeanor instantly silenced the murmurs of the crowd.

Mikael stepped forward, but before he could say anything, the man said, "Ah, the tireless Vasilakis. No rest until you've saved the world, eh?" A murmur went through the crowd, followed by indignant shouts. Mikael sensed the tension intensifying.

"Mr. Leonard, we are here because the government has failed. We are demanding our right to clean air. We won't leave until our voices have been heard."

Leonard stepped even closer, his face now only a few inches from Mikael's. "You're endangering lives here. The air quality is particularly bad today, and your protest is putting more people at risk."

Mikael was not intimidated. "We are in danger every day when we breathe this polluted air. We risk our lives because the government does nothing. If you're truly concerned, ensure our demands are met."

Leonard poked Mikael in the chest. "Final warning, Vasilakis: Clear the square, or we'll be forced to take action."

"Yes, take action! Actions that will end the Gray Winter!" Mikael shouted, and a loud cheer broke out among the protesters.

Leonard gave a frustrated signal, and the security forces withdrew. "This isn't over, Vasilakis." He turned and walked away.

Mikael watched Leonard leave and knew the fight indeed was far from over. However, this small victory gave him new strength and confidence.

He turned again to the protesters and raised the megaphone. "Friends, we've made our message clear. It's not safe to stay here longer. Let's withdraw for now, but our fighting spirit remains unbroken! We'll return, stronger and more determined than ever!" The crowd cheered, and Mikael felt deep satisfaction. Today's protest had garnered the attention he had hoped for.

As the demonstrators rolled up their banners, a young man with a sturdy build and traces of earth on his clothing approached. It was Samuel, a farmer's son, whose expression, despite his visible exhaustion, revealed an unyielding willpower. His eyes were reddened, and his voice trembled as he began to speak: "Mikael, I can't leave without telling you how important this fight is for me. My father and I work hard on our farm, but we see that our harvests are getting worse because of the polluted air. It's really affecting us." He paused briefly, seemingly trying to collect himself before continuing. "The fight you're leading here today is also our fight—the fight of all who suffer from air pollution. Thank you for speaking for us, even when no one appears to want to hear us."

Mikael placed his hand on Samuel's shoulder. He felt compassion, and it was important to him to show his appreciation. "My friend, it's I who should be the one offering thanks. It's courageous people like you who remind me why we must not give up this fight. We'll keep going—for you, your father, and all who suffer from this crisis."

Just as they were symbolically laying down some banners in front of the government building, they heard sirens in the distance. *Leonard has apparently alerted the police.* Mikael felt increasing tension, and the protesters exchanged worried glances. With a calming gesture, he raised his hand. "Go now, before the police get here."

The remaining protesters hesitated, but Mikael's determined tone spurred them on. "Let's stay calm and leave the square in an orderly fashion. We've made our point."

The sirens grew louder, and shortly thereafter, several police vehicles appeared at the edge of the square. Officers got out and quickly formed up, ready to disperse the crowd by force if necessary. Their determined expressions and riot gear signaled that they were prepared for any form of resistance. Mikael observed the scenario and knew this was a critical moment.

"Friends, leave slowly and peacefully," he repeated firmly. "Let's show that we don't want conflict or escalation. We act responsibly."

The protesters began to withdraw gradually, with some casting final defiant glances at the approaching officers. Just as Mikael was about to turn around, he felt a policeman seize his arm and pull him aside. "That's it. You're coming with us." Mikael felt the cold handcuffs snap around his wrists; a shiver ran down his spine.

At that moment, the situation escalated. Some protesters rushed back to defend Mikael. Immediately, a violent scuffle broke out. The police used tear gas, and a biting cloud rose into the air. The crowd's protective masks weren't enough to prevent the vapors from penetrating their masks, causing them to cough, rubbing their teary eyes, they did not retreat.

The officers dragged Mikael toward a police car, but the crowd became denser and louder. They eventually formed a human chain around Mikael to protect him. An officer pushed one of the protesters to the ground, while another struck him with his baton. "Stick together!" Mikael shouted defiantly as he desperately kicked against the officers. "Don't let them intimidate you!"

He found himself amidst the now rampant chaos, surrounded by police and protesters. The handcuffs cut painfully into his wrists, hindering his movements. He planted his feet and roared, "We fight for our rights!"

Suddenly, he felt a heavy blow from behind. He stumbled forward, but before he could regain his balance, a strike hit him full in the face. Pain exploded in his head; his vision blurred, and he couldn't see who had hit him.

"You may drive us away today, but—" He didn't get any further, as he lost consciousness.

When Mikael came to, he felt dazed and disoriented. His hands were still cuffed behind his back; he was lying on the hard backseat of a moving police car. His face throbbed with pain, and the metallic ringing in his ears made the tumult of the demonstration seem like a distant echo.

CHAPTER 6
YOUNG ADULTS –
THE JOURNEY BEGINS

On a dreary afternoon not long after the demonstration, a group of teenagers sneaked into an abandoned warehouse on the outskirts of the city. Water dripped from the ceiling, highlighting the neglected state of the place, and colorful graffiti with climate slogans covered the walls. The occasional creaking of the dilapidated wooden roof repeatedly broke the oppressive silence. The musty smell of damp concrete and old oil hung heavily in the air, intensifying their frustration of the situation in Plainfield. The recent cancellation of football training had been a hard blow for the group. Despite the worsening air quality, their strict coach had insisted on training outdoors, but concerned parents and community voices opposed this, and the training was eventually halted for safety reasons. This showed how far-reaching the environmental crisis was affecting their lives. Football was more than just a sport; it was a vent for stress, a source of team spirit, and a piece of normalcy.

"I've had enough, guys!" shouted Alex, the leader of the group. With restless eyes and clenched fists, he looked like a volcano about to erupt. "We're wasting our youth!" His voice trembled with anger as he recalled the many evenings in his room, overwhelmed by boredom and lack of prospects while the smog outside darkened the city. With an angry kick against the warehouse wall, he let his despair run free.

"Wow!" exclaimed Lara, Alex's girlfriend, suddenly staring at her mobile phone. Her blue eyes widened as a strand of her long blonde hair fell into her face. With her flawless appearance, she would have been the undisputed beauty of the school—but due to digital classes, that hardly came into play. "Come here and look at this—the video is going viral!" Immediately, the friends gathered around her. On the screen, a young man was walking under a bright blue sky through a lush green landscape. Birds chirped; the sun shone on vibrant grass.

"Here in the south, you can breathe freely." He spread his arms and took a deep breath. "No smog clouds, no toxic fumes—just fresh air that invigorates the lungs and frees the heart. I'm Tim from SouthHope, and I'm showing you how beautiful it is here. But that's not all. We're collecting donations for reforestation and the protection of this unique landscape. Every contribution helps. Follow me and share this video. We are the future!"

The friends stared spellbound at the screen. Lara's usually talkative mouth hung open. "That's really impressive," she murmured, her eyes glistening.

"My brother moved south last year. He says the air is somewhat better, but this video... wow, it looks like a different world!" said Tom thoughtfully. With his calm manner and deep brown eyes, he often seemed like the rock of the group. Of average height, with short light brown hair, his friendly, open face made him appear more likable than traditionally handsome.

Alex scoffed. "That doesn't help us here. Plainfield really stinks."

Naomi, a whirlwind of energy and with an infectious smile, ran her hand through her cheeky pixie haircut and grinned challengingly. "What are we waiting for? Let's head south!"

Lara raised her eyebrows, surprised by Naomi's enthusiasm. "What do you mean?"

Naomi hesitated briefly and thought. A car was out of the question these days. The bus and train network was so severely restricted that they couldn't rely on it either. Suddenly, her face lit up. "We'll go by bike—environmentally friendly and flexible! Thanks to our football training, we're perfectly prepared," she explained excitedly, looking at the others hopefully.

The teenagers exchanged meaningful glances. Alex's anger transformed into a contemplative expression. "We've got nothing to lose. We can't go on like this."

"Good idea," whispered Lara. "It's unbearable at home. There are five of us in a tiny apartment, and my father... drinks too much. I just want to get away." Alex pulled her into a loving embrace.

Basil, always ready for an adventure, approached the group with determined steps. His dark, slightly tousled hair peeked out from under a baseball cap, and beneath the plastic protective suit, he wore a loose hoodie that was too big for him—only enhancing his relaxed, carefree aura. A mischievous grin revealed he had a joke on his lips. Without hesitation, he stretched out his hand. "Where can I sign up?" His positive energy swept over the whole group, and soon they couldn't suppress smiles behind their masks.

The teenagers immediately began preparations. Alex mapped out the route while Lara and Naomi gathered survival gear. Tom checked the air quality, and Basil rummaged through old boxes in the warehouse, finding useful tools and spare parts for their bicycles. After a period of intense planning and preparation, they had organized the essentials. The young people were ready to embark on their journey into the unknown—even if not everything was perfect yet.

"Hey, what if we film everything, like that guy from SouthHope?" Tom sounded excited. "We can document it all and show the unvarnished truth, but also the hopeful moments. We could really make a difference, guys. Imagine—we wouldn't just be witnesses but also ambassadors for a better future." He looked at the others eagerly, who slowly nodded as they grasped the magnitude of his vision.

Lara grabbed her mobile phone, a smile playing on her lips. "You know, I've made a lot of videos for social networks," she explained to the group. "I know how to film, edit, and upload everything. Let's use that to share our journey. I'll create a new channel tonight where we can post all our experiences."

The group gathered around Lara, all enthusiastic about sharing their story.

"We need a cool name for the channel," said Tom thoughtfully. "Something that shows what we stand for and what we hope for."

"How about *Breathing Paths*?" suggested Naomi. "It fits our search for fresh air and shows that we're making our own way."

"I'm for *Fresh Air Fanatics*," joked Basil. "It shows that we seriously need fresh air. Plus, it's a bit of fun!"

"I like *Exploring Horizons*," said Lara. "It's about more than just clean air. It's about exploring new horizons and showing what's beyond the pollution."

Finally, by a show of hands, the group decided on *Exploring Horizons*. Lara nodded with satisfaction and immediately began designing the profile and layout of the channel.

With a loud crash, the warehouse door flew open. A broad-shouldered man stormed in, his eyes blazing with anger. "What the hell are you doing here?" he bellowed.

The teenagers froze in shock. Only Alex was capable of reacting. "Who are you anyway?"

"I'm the owner of this warehouse," the man growled. "You have no business here. Go home immediately—the air is deadly!" The teenagers looked at each other silently.

"Out, or I'll call the police!" the man shouted. The group exchanged nervous glances, their body language reflecting the sudden tension. Alex wanted to stand up, his nostrils flaring with anger, but Lara was quicker and grabbed his arm.

"Okay, let's go," she said calmly before he could say anything. "We're setting off early tomorrow. Don't forget your bikes."

The teenagers made moves to leave, but the man raised his hand. "Wait! Where are you going?" They hesitated, exchanging glances again.

"South," murmured Naomi finally.

The man stepped closer, fixing them sharply. "South? Why?"

"The air quality is better," said Lara quietly. "We've heard that it's easier to breathe there."

"You really believe that and want to just head south on bicycles?" the man asked incredulously. Lara nodded uncertainly.

"Are you out of your minds? We're in the middle of the Gray Winter. Do you know how dangerous that is?" He looked at each of the teenagers, aghast.

Alex stepped forward, hands on hips. "We're tired of just sitting around. The air here is making us sick. We have to find out if it's better elsewhere."

"You're crazy!" The man's threatening tone gave way to concern. "I'll call your parents! They'll flip when they hear this. You could seriously put yourselves in danger!"

"You don't know our parents," countered Basil firmly but nervously.

The man shook his head, needing to cough heavily before he could respond. He raised a finger of warning. "You're risking your lives." He then left the warehouse.

An oppressive silence prevailed. Naomi was visibly upset. "Is he right? Are we just naive? Maybe we're underestimating what this really means."

"It's easier to sit here and freeze in panic," Alex responded. "The life we want is waiting out there. We must not let our fear paralyze us, and we certainly should not be intimidated by an old, frustrated man."

The discussion heated up, with Alex urging them to set off immediately, while Naomi cautioned for prudence. Lara thought about the bad circumstances at home. She definitely wanted to leave. Basil rubbed his chin thoughtfully, torn between the allure of an adventure before starting his studies and the worry of leaving his family behind.

"Let's flip a coin. Heads, we go. Tails, we wait a bit longer," suggested Tom. The others exchanged looks. Finally, they nodded. Tom tossed the coin into the air, and they all watched its flight intently. It landed on heads.

Basil raised his fist and called out firmly, "For freedom!" His eyes sparkled with resolve. The others looked at him, still hesitant. Uncertainty lay in their faces. Sensing their reluctance, Basil took a step forward and called out louder, "For freedom!" His voice echoed throughout the warehouse, filling every corner, his burning gaze urging his friends to join him.

For a moment, there was silence. Then Lara slowly raised her fist and shouted, "For freedom!"

Alex followed with an even stronger voice, "For freedom!"

One after the other, the teenagers joined in until their united shouts made the warehouse tremble. "For freedom! For freedom!"

Naomi looked around the group. "What about our parents? We can't just take off without letting them know."

"We'll leave a message," suggested Tom. "An explanation so they know why we're gone and that we'll keep in touch. We'll include the name of our channel so they can follow us and see what we're experiencing."

"Perfect," said Alex. "Let's do it that way."

In the cool dawn of the next morning, Alex, Lara, Naomi, Tom, and Basil met again. Each had a backpack and their bicycle. The group was both excited and tense. Their journey would be physically and emotionally demanding. Despite the uncertainty, determination shone in their eyes.

Lara pulled out her mobile phone and activated the camera. Alex stepped forward, his expression serious, the stern look revealing his resolve. "Hey to everyone following us on Exploring Horizons. We're leaving Plainfield in search of clean air and with the goal of making a statement. This here," he said, pointing to the fog, "is the result of years of neglect. Our journey aims to prove that there are still places where living in harmony with nature is possible, and to show that together we can change the future."

Lara slowly panned the camera over the group; every face reflected courage and conviction. Then she directed the lens at the road ahead of them, which disappeared into fog softly illuminated by the first light of the rising sun.

"We don't know what's ahead of us," Alex continued. "But we know that each of us is determined to find a better future—not just for ourselves but for all who will follow."

Naomi stepped in front of the camera; her eyes sparkled with excitement. "This is our message to the world," she said with a smile. "The circumstances are difficult, but our will is unwavering. We're heading south in search of a place where we can breathe freely again. And we'll share every experience, every encounter, and every moment with you, so you understand that giving up is not an option."

With a final look into the camera, Lara added, "Follow us on Exploring Horizons to share in our progress and our stories. This is the beginning of a new chapter." When the recording was finished, she stowed the mobile phone, and they mounted their bicycles. The soft hum of the wheels broke the silence as they left their past behind with every turn of the pedals and moved toward an unknown, hopefully better future.

Their journey led them through abandoned suburbs and overgrown fields. The cold bit into their faces and made their fingers numb. They saw the devastating effects of the emissions everywhere: poisoned soils, destroyed crops, stretches of land where nothing grew anymore. In small villages, the few remaining inhabitants peeked suspiciously from behind dusty curtains. With each kilometer they covered, the extent of the crisis became clearer to them.

Dusk settled over the country road, and an icy wind blew through the bare trees lining it. Exhausted from the long ride, they decided to stop close to a desolate village.

Alex sank into the damp grass and stared into the distance, where the fog seemed to swallow the world. The others joined him, each lost in their thoughts. After a few minutes, Naomi broke the silence. "It's sad to see all this," she whispered. "Yet I feel more alive than ever."

Lara nodded thoughtfully and pulled out her mobile phone. "Let's capture the first day," she suggested. "After that, we should look for a sheltered place to sleep."

The friends huddled close together to fit into the frame. The

warm light of the setting sun bathed their faces in golden tones—
a sharp contrast to the gloomy surroundings. Lara started the
recording.

"Hey, everyone out there," Alex began firmly. "Today we've
seen more than destroyed landscapes. We've seen what happens
when we do nothing."

Naomi took over, her eyes sparkling with determination.
"We've met people who, despite everything, don't give up hope.
That gives us the strength to keep going."

Tom picked a withered piece of grass. "This was once a
blooming field. We must not allow our world to end like this."

Basil continued, "The first day of our journey was hard, but it
has shown us how necessary it is. For us, for you, for everyone."

Lara panned the camera over the barren, desolate landscape.
"This is our reality, but we believe in a better future. And we
won't stop until we find it," she added, before ending the
recording.

"Hey, someone's coming," Alex said, standing up. The others
followed his gaze.

An older man in worn-out clothing and with a glass eye
emerged from the fog, his movements slow and deliberate. "I
heard you talking," he said in a rough voice. "What you're doing
is brave. If you want, you can find shelter at my place for the
night. It's getting cold."

Naomi felt an icy shiver run down her spine. She couldn't
stop looking at his glass eye. "That's kind, but we'll manage," she
said quickly.

Tom glanced at her in surprise before addressing the man.
"Actually, that would be very helpful," he replied. "Thank you
very much!"

"Well then, follow me," the man said. He turned without
acknowledging Naomi's concerns.

Alex packed up his things and grinned. "A roof over our
heads doesn't sound bad at all. Perfect end to the first day."

The teenagers followed the man, who introduced himself as
Graham, along a narrow, bumpy road to his house. As night fell,
it became bitterly cold, and the temperature seemed to keep

dropping.

Suddenly, Naomi pulled Lara aside. "Something's not right with him," she whispered. "Did you see his glass eye? And how he was watching us?"

Lara shrugged. "He's probably just a lonely old man. Don't be so suspicious. We need a place to sleep."

When they entered Graham's modest house, he lit several candles that bathed the room in warm, flickering light.

"Don't you have electricity?" Tom asked, surprised. He glanced around the dimly lit room. Simple wooden furniture and a sofa with worn upholstery testified to a sparse life.

Graham shrugged. "Sometimes we have power, but it usually goes out in the evenings. We've gotten used to candles."

An uneasy feeling crept over Naomi as she stepped inside. The flickering candles cast eerie shadows on the walls, and a musty smell intensified her discomfort.

The teenagers sat on rustic wooden benches around the table while Graham served bread and cheese. "You must be hungry. Help yourselves."

"Thank you very much," Lara said sincerely. "Would you like to tell the people in Plainfield something? We're making videos of our journey to show what it's really like out here."

Graham hesitated for a moment, then nodded. "Perhaps it's time city folks learn how we're doing."

Lara pulled out her mobile phone while Graham took a small comb from his pocket and straightened his hair. Smoothing his shirt, he then he gave Lara a signal. They began.

"Out here in the countryside, everything is different to the city," he started in a low voice. "Power outages are part of daily life. In the evenings, there's often no light, no hot water. The old air purifiers we have barely work anymore." He pointed to a dusty device in the corner. "And you'd better not drink the tap water."

Naomi felt something change within her. Maybe she had judged him too quickly.

The teenagers listened attentively as Graham continued. "We often feel forgotten. Many have moved away, and those who stayed are struggling to survive. There are no doctors here anymore, and if someone gets sick, we're on our own. Despite everything, we stick together. We share the little we have. That's our way of defying the Gray Winter."

Lara ended the recording, and an odd silence filled the room. The teenagers looked around and realized how hard life was here—and yet they felt the warmth Graham exuded despite all adversity.

"Thank you for sharing that with us," Lara finally said softly.

Graham gave a faint smile. "Maybe it will make a difference."

"We'll make sure it reaches many people," promised Alex.

"Get some rest," Graham said as he stood up. "You have a long journey ahead."

The teenagers lay down on the simple mattresses Graham provided. While the others soon fell into an exhausted sleep, Naomi lay awake. She thought about the evening. Graham had helped them even though he had so little. His friendly smile and the warmth in his eyes—even in the glass one—made her reconsider her reservations.

The shadows of the candles danced on the ceiling, and the silence of the night was overwhelming. Naomi felt her unease gradually turn into compassion. She could see that the people here in the countryside were different to city folks. Community seemed to have a deeper value. A sense of gratitude washed over her. Perhaps this journey was teaching her more than she ever expected. Finally, she fell into a deep, restful sleep.

CHAPTER 7
FAMILY HAWKINS –
THE FARM ON THE OUTSKIRTS

Thomas Hawkins stood at the edge of his field, his hands buried deep in the pockets of his worn denim jacket. His gaze swept over the endless rows of barren earth where once a variety of vegetables had thrived. Now the soil lay lifeless under a leaden gray sky. The weak wind barely managed to move the toxic haze over the land. The earth, which had once been their livelihood, now appeared bare and parched.

The breathing mask bothered him, so he pushed it under his chin to breathe freely again—as freely as the polluted air allowed. A bitter smell of chemicals rose to his nose, and a metallic taste settled on his tongue, but that didn't seem to concern Thomas. He wanted to feel the air of his land, experienced without the barrier between himself and the world he knew.

Beside him stood his eldest son, Samuel, wrapped in the protective gear the government recommended. His face was hidden behind a breathing mask, but his eyes reflected concern.

"Father, you should really take this more seriously. Where are your gloves?" Samuel asked reproachfully. He pointed to Thomas's bare hands. "The soil is poisoned, you know that. Any contact can be dangerous."

Thomas gave him a defiant look. "I don't need plastic between me and my land," he replied sharply. He dug his right hand deep into the cool, crumbly soil, as if he could retrieve the lost vitality. "I want to feel the earth, like before."

Samuel sighed and stepped closer. "But times have changed. It's about your health. Think of me and Mother."

Thomas closed his fist around a handful of dry earth, so tightly that it trickled between his fingers. "This land has fed our family for generations," he said quietly. "I won't become estranged from it." He felt alive when he touched the earth—as if it were a part of him, the last hold in a world that was inexorably changing.

Samuel watched his father with concern. "Father, the air pollution is dangerous. You should wear the protective clothing," he tried again.

Thomas looked at his son. A faint smile flitted across his lips, but he couldn't hide the worry in his eyes. "I know, my boy, but some things must remain as they've always been. Without direct contact with the earth, we're not real farmers." Samuel sighed and finally relented. He knew he couldn't change his father's mind. At least Thomas was now wearing a breathing mask—a concession in itself.

Both looked at the sad rows of earth mounds where their latest cultivation project, a variety of root vegetables, was growing—or supposed to be growing.

"We've changed everything, Father, as they advised us. Potatoes, carrots, even beets, but look at this," said Samuel. He pulled a young carrot from the ground, whose pale, shriveled surface revealed its desperate struggle for survival. "Even underground, they're struggling."

Thomas nodded. Since the government's advice to switch to root vegetables, the family had completely changed their cultivation strategy. Root vegetables were more robust and less susceptible to the pollutants that poisoned the air and desolated the soil. They needed less light compared to other varieties, an invaluable advantage in this gloomy world. All the more painful was the sight of the meager harvest.

"It's the air," murmured Thomas, almost like a prayer. "Even the most fertile soil can't do anything if the breath of the earth is poisoned." His voice reflected pain and lost hope.

Since international trade had been restricted, each region had to largely feed itself, which increased the pressure on local farmers. The Hawkins family had hoped that the switch would help them meet the quotas set by the government—the minimum amount of food that each farm had to contribute to supply the cities. Despite their hard work, the yields were declining.

Thomas crouched down and ran his hand over the ground. For generations, this soil had been the pride of his family. "You see, Sam," he said, directing his gaze at the infertile soil, "this land fed your grandfather and your great-grandfather, just as it feeds us. They cared for it with traditional methods, always in harmony with nature." His voice was firm, but there was a hint of wistfulness in his eyes. "From them, I learned to read the signs of the earth—how it breathes, how it reacts. These new indoor systems can't replace the feeling you get when you work directly with the earth. This is our life's work. The technologies alienate us from what agriculture really means."

In the evening, after dinner, father and son were still sitting at the kitchen table while Mrs. Hawkins was doing the dishes. The boy took a deep breath.

"Father, we need to talk."

Thomas looked up, his eyes narrowed and full of hardness. "If it's again about that damn indoor system, you can spare your words."

"But you see that it can't go on like this! Our harvests are shrinking, we no longer meet the government's quotas, and the bills are piling up." Samuel struck the table with his palm. "We have to change something before it's too late."

Thomas stood up abruptly, the chair clattering to the floor behind him. "I won't allow machines to replace my fields! This land is our life, not some factory." For him, the land was more than just soil and plants—it was their history, their heritage. But the worries in his son's eyes moved him, and inwardly he was torn.

Samuel also stood up, tears of anger glistening in his eyes. "And what if soon there's no land left, and we lose everything just because you're too stubborn to change?" He felt a mixture of frustration and compassion. Why couldn't his father understand that he only wanted the best for them? If they continued like this, they would be ruined.

The words hung heavily in the air. Thomas's face froze, and without another word, he left the room. Samuel remained alone in the oppressive silence.

The next morning, while Thomas and Samuel were cleaning the potato harvester in the barn, Mrs. Hawkins came up to them. "There's someone from the Ministry of Agriculture on the phone." With a grim expression, Thomas went back into the house; Samuel followed him wordlessly.

"Hawkins here," grumbled Thomas into the phone.

At the other end of the line, a female official spoke: "We need to talk about your current production figures. You are significantly below the prescribed quotas." Her voice was so loud and clear that Samuel could hear every word.

"How about you come over? Do you have any idea the conditions under which we're working here?" Thomas felt his blood begin to boil.

"We are aware of the situation," the official replied coolly. "If you continue to be unable to meet your quotas, we will be forced to cut government support."

"You can go to hell!" Thomas burst out.

Samuel hastily stepped forward and took the receiver from his hand. "This is Samuel Hawkins. The situation is more complicated than it appears on paper. We've implemented all recommendations, but the yields are still lacking. The soil is too heavily contaminated."

"Mr. Hawkins, the guidelines already take these factors into account. The quota was individually adjusted to the size of your farm. Other farms are meeting the quotas without problems."

"With all due respect," Samuel replied calmly, "many of these farms have indoor systems. Without this technology, it's practically impossible to produce the required amounts.”

“Then you should seriously consider it,” the official said in a matter-of-fact tone. “The funding is available but comes with conditions. If the quotas continue not to be met, we will be forced to recoup those costs, which would potentially lead to the forfeiture of your land.”

Samuel pressed his lips together. “I understand. We will review our options.”

“Do that,” she replied firmly. “Good day.”

After he hung up, there was a moment of oppressive silence. Thomas’s face was flushed with anger. “These bureaucrats have no idea! Sitting in their offices and making our lives difficult.”

Samuel took a deep breath. “Father, they’ve warned us, and not for the first time. If we don’t meet the quotas, we’ll lose the subsidies. Without them, we can’t manage.”

Thomas slammed his fist on the table. “I won’t be blackmailed! We’ve done everything they wanted, and still, it’s not enough for them.”

“It’s not us, but the conditions,” Samuel replied calmly. “The soil is poisoned, the air polluted. Our traditional methods no longer work.”

Thomas turned away and stared out the window. “I won’t give up my land. Not for some sterile factory hall where soulless plants are grown.”

Samuel stepped next to him. “If we don’t change anything now, soon there will be no land left for you to fight for. I will submit the application for the indoor system—with or without your support.”

The following days were marked by icy silence. At breakfast, Thomas and Samuel sat opposite each other, but neither spoke a word. Mrs. Hawkins, noticing the tense situation, tried in vain several times to start a conversation. Samuel spent hours in his room, engrossed in documents and sketches, while Thomas desperately continued to work outside to save the harvest. Despite all efforts, he couldn’t prevent the yields from remaining meager.

On the day of the application hearing, Samuel was nervous.

His heart pounded as he entered the meeting room. The cool stares of the committee members rested on him. He took a deep breath and began his presentation. His voice trembled slightly at first, but the longer he spoke about the project, the more confident he became. He showed sketches, explained the advantages of the indoor system, and outlined how they intended to meet the quotas with it. With clear, well-founded arguments, he answered the committee members' questions. When he finished, there was a pause until the chairman nodded appreciatively.

"Mr. Hawkins," the chairman said, "your presentation is convincing. We see the potential of your project and are willing to support it."

Relief washed over Samuel, but at the same time, he felt a slight pang of doubt. Would his father ever accept it?

On the way home, his thoughts revolved around the impending conversation. He arrived to find Thomas on the porch, without a breathing mask, his hands tightly clasped around a steaming cup of tea. The steam rose in small wisps. Samuel approached him, unsure of how to begin.

"Father," he said quietly.

Thomas did not look up. "How did it go?" he asked tonelessly.

"The authorities agreed," Samuel said calmly. "The indoor facility is coming."

A long silence followed. Thomas took a sip of tea, his gaze still directed into the distance. "So, you've had your way."

Samuel sensed the underlying reproach in his words. "I'm doing this for all of us. For the farm, for our future."

Thomas sighed deeply, as if a heavy weight lay upon him. "Maybe I just don't understand the world anymore." He stood up, took his cup, and slowly went into the house without looking at Samuel again. "Do what you think is right."

Before Samuel could reply, the door closed softly behind his father. He remained alone; the weight of his decision now rested heavier than ever on his shoulders.

In the following weeks, the farm transformed into a bustling construction site. Trucks delivered materials; the pounding of hammers and the humming of machines filled the air. Samuel worked tirelessly, often late into the night, sleeves rolled up, sweat on his forehead. He supervised the installation of the air filtration systems, adjusted the growth lamps, and checked every detail to ensure everything ran perfectly.

Thomas watched him from a distance. At first, he held back, unsure of how to involve himself in this new chapter of the family business. But the more he saw how much Samuel was striving, the clearer it became that his son's commitment sprang from the same love for the land that had always driven him.

One afternoon, Samuel found his father in the barn, cleaning old tools. "Father, I could use your help," Samuel said hesitantly.

Thomas looked up. "With what?"

"The sensors for humidity control need to be installed. Your experience would be really helpful."

Thomas wiped his hands on an old cloth and finally nodded. "Alright, then I'll show you young technicians how to do it properly."

Side by side, they worked together. Old and new methods merged as Thomas contributed his practical knowledge and Samuel explained the modern technologies. The initial tension between them began to dissolve, replaced by a shared goal.

One evening, as the sun disappeared behind the hills and the indoor facility was bathed in soft, warm light, father and son stood side by side, looking at the first tender plants sprouting under the lamps. Thomas broke the silence. "Maybe you're right, Samuel. Maybe this is our way forward."

Those words meant more to Samuel than all the subsidies combined. They were the affirmation he had long hoped for—the proof that his father trusted him. He put his arm around his father's shoulders. "We'll make it, Father. Together."

CHAPTER 8
CLARA ZHENG –
HEAD OF INNOTECH

As dusk settled over the city and the dense gray smog swallowed the last traces of daylight, the lights in the ultramodern offices of InnoTech were still burning. Clara Zheng, the founder and driving force behind the startup, stood motionless at the window, staring into the blurred silhouette of the city. Her sleek black hair was tied into an elegant bun, emphasizing her high cheekbones and the clear lines of her face. Her company was her life's work—a pioneer in the fight against the Gray Winter.

The only decoration in the minimalist office was an artistic calligraphy depicting the character for harmony or peace, a gift from her grandmother upon her graduation.

The shrill ringing of the phone shattered the silence. With a calm, controlled movement, Clara reached for the headset and answered the call.

"Good evening, Ms. Zheng. This is the Ministry of Environment and Energy. Recent reports and protests regarding the sharp acceleration in air pollution require urgent action. Dr. Vogel from the Institute of Environmental Technology and Climate Research has pointed out the dramatic deterioration of air quality. We must prevent an escalation at all costs."

Clara sat down; her full attention was on the conversation. "How can I help?"

"Your company is a leader in the development of air filtration technologies and has made a name for itself far beyond Plainfield. That's why we're reaching out to you. We are prepared to fully support your project. Costs are not an issue at this stage."

Adrenaline coursed through Clara. She felt the pressure and expectations, but also the unbridled desire to finally make her visions a reality. This was the moment she and her team had been working toward. "Thank you for your trust," she said firmly. "We have already made significant progress in developing a new technology that not only cleans the air but also drastically reduces emissions, and we are ready to take on the challenge."

"That sounds promising," the official replied. "But time is ticking. The public expects quick results. How soon can you deliver?"

Clara felt the invisible pressure of time. "Our prototypes have already shown impressive lab results. We plan to begin field tests in the next few days and expect initial positive outcomes within three to six months."

"Three to six months?" The disappointment in the government representative's voice was unmistakable. "I'm afraid that's too long, Ms. Zheng. Is there no way to speed up the process? The situation is getting more serious every day."

"We are already working at full capacity," Clara assured, internally reviewing her resources. "With additional experts and simplified approvals for the tests, we could significantly shorten the time."

"Alright," the official said after a brief pause. "I'll ensure you have the necessary resources at your disposal. Please keep us regularly updated on your progress."

"Understood," Clara replied calmly, even though she felt the weight of responsibility. "You can count on us."

She set down the headset and paused for a moment in silent reflection. *Less than three to six months... Is that really feasible?* She knew that the team was already working at its limit. As she intensely considered the next steps, a determined smile formed on her lips. *This is the breakthrough we've been waiting for.* Without hesitation, she turned to her computer and called the team to an urgent meeting. Her movements were precise—the movements of a woman who not only accepted great challenges but mastered them.

When Clara entered the conference room, all eyes instantly turned to her. An expectant tension hung in the air. "We are at a critical milestone," Clara began with a firm, clear voice, fully aware of her charismatic presence. "The government has given our project the green light and promised us additional resources. This is our chance not only to elevate InnoTech to the next level but also to gain global recognition and sustainably change the world."

Clara let her gaze wander over the faces of her employees—the young engineers full of fresh ideas and enthusiasm, alongside experienced colleagues whose wrinkles and gray strands testified to decades of hard work. "Our mission is clear. We are developing a technology that cleans the air and drastically reduces emissions. Is there anyone new on the team who is not yet familiar with the details of our technology?"

Simon Carson, a young engineer who had been seconded from the Institute of Environmental Technology and Climate Research to contribute his expertise during this critical phase, hesitantly raised his hand. "Excuse me, yes, I'm still getting up to speed on the biotechnological aspects. Could you please briefly explain how the technology works exactly?"

Clara smiled understandingly. "Of course. Our technology is based on a multi-layered nanomembrane that, together with special catalytic processes, efficiently filters pollutants from the air and converts them into harmless compounds. The first layer binds particles like nitrogen oxides and sulfur dioxide. The second ensures that these are stably bound, while the third layer is coated with catalysts to transform the pollutants into harmless substances like nitrate salts and zinc sulfites. Our tests have shown that the technology can reduce pollutant levels by up to 70 percent, significantly improving air quality."

Dr. Bruno Hansen, an engineer with unruly hair and glasses that constantly slipped down his nose, nodded in agreement. "That's truly impressive, Clara. What are the next steps?"

"Field tests," Clara replied decisively. "We need to ensure that the technology works just as efficiently outside the lab. Once we've gathered enough data, we'll begin mass production. Thanks to government support and simplified approvals, we can significantly speed up the process."

Her eyes gleamed with excitement as she said, "A challenging time lies ahead, but I have full confidence in all of you." She added emphatically, "Our goal is to make this technology available worldwide and sustainably improve air quality."

The moment had come to prove what InnoTech could achieve. The team was aware of the gigantic task, but under Clara's visionary leadership, no one doubted their ability to meet its demands. "Let's not see this crisis merely as a threat but also as an opportunity—an opportunity to show the world what science and innovation can accomplish."

Back at her desk, Clara immersed herself in work on her laptop. The cold blue light of the screen cast a contemplative glow on her face as she entered the new parameters into the project plan. "With these additional funds," she murmured softly, absentmindedly biting her lower lip, "we can immediately hire more experts, accelerate development, and expand the testing phases." The new, aggressive schedule would force her to start processes in parallel. *Managing risks while moving forward quickly.* She reread the words she had just recorded in the plan. Clara was aware of the enormous challenge but would not have come this far in her career if she gave up easily.

With the next steps firmly in mind, Clara called her core team together again. "I have a plan that will allow us to use the additional resources effectively and accelerate our project. We need to tighten schedules and can't waste a second. With the financial and political support of the government, we'll succeed."

Clara sketched the shortened timeline on the whiteboard. The marker made a scratching sound as it moved across the surface. She listed the new resources available to them. "Each of you will have to take on more responsibility. Our goal is to complete prototyping and testing phases in a fraction of the originally planned time."

The team members exchanged glances; some appeared hesitant, furrowing their brows, others nodded resolutely.

Dr. Bruno Hansen cleared his throat and broke the silence. "Clara, I understand the pressure we're under," he began cautiously, "but I'm worried that by shortening the testing phases, we're taking risks we can't fully assess."

Clara met his gaze; her eyes searched his. "What exactly are your concerns?"

He took a deep breath. "If we rush the tests, we might overlook potential errors or issues. Our technology is complex, and on such a large scale, even small inconsistencies can have significant impacts."

A soft murmur went through the room; some team members nodded in agreement, others looked thoughtful.

Clara paused and let Bruno Hansen's words sink in for a moment. "Your point is valid," she finally admitted. "We have to find a way to work more efficiently without compromising quality and safety." She looked around. "Does anyone have ideas on how we can resolve this dilemma?"

Bruno Hansen spoke up again. "What if we outsource part of the testing to trusted partners—companies that already have experience in these areas? I could establish some contacts. That would relieve some of the pressure on us while ensuring the necessary diligence."

Clara nodded as she weighed up the idea. "That could be a solution. If we distribute the tests across multiple shoulders, we can focus on the core areas. We'll look into it."

The tense atmosphere in the room began to gradually ease, and the team members animatedly exchanged ideas about the next steps. Clara knew it was no easy task, but under this pressure, she thrived—and so did the team.

Simon Carson added, "For the testing phases, we could rely more on simulations. We'd need to bring IT experts onto the team for that. With their help, we could run through complex scenarios virtually, and identify potential problems early on. That way, we wouldn't have to shorten the real tests too much and would still have control over quality."

Bruno Hansen nodded. "If we carefully decide which tasks to outsource and ensure that our partners adhere to the quality standards, that could work. The simulations could accelerate the most critical tests without us having to forgo thorough analyses."

Clara smiled with relief. "Those are excellent suggestions. We can use the additional funding to hire experienced partners for testing and new IT experts for simulations. That way, we speed up the process without taking risks."

The atmosphere was now noticeably more relaxed, and a new energy flowed through the team as they began focusing on implementing the ideas.

"Good," Clara said decisively. "Let's distribute the tasks. Lisa, please take care of identifying potential partner companies and drafting the contracts. Simon, you'll lead the simulation team and ensure we make optimal use of the IT resources. Bruno, I want you to oversee quality assurance and make sure all external work meets our standards."

The team members nodded, their eyes shining with new confidence.

Clara chose her next words carefully. "We're not just developing a technology here—we have the most advanced solution to end this crisis. The world is watching us." She paused briefly, letting the moment sink in, and then added with firm conviction, "I know that together we can achieve great things."

With renewed vigor, the team set to work. Clara stayed in the office long into the night, planning the next steps and coordinating workflows. It was already just before midnight when she stood up and went to the window to grant herself a brief break.

Can I risk shortening the testing phases? What if something goes wrong? The thoughts circled in her head, but the dense smog reminded her that delays were not an option. Her eyes narrowed. *Strange, I can usually see all the way to the street.*

An unsettling feeling rose within her, and a cold shiver ran down her spine. *I know exactly what that means.*

CHAPTER 9
PLAINFIELD –
BREATHLESS

The city suffocated under an eternal twilight as the environmental monitor incessantly glowed a deep violet—an alarming warning color signaling the escalation of the Gray Winter. Air quality had now reached a dangerous low point. Hospitals, once safe havens, were bursting at the seams, overwhelmed by the steadily growing number of patients with severe respiratory problems.

At St. Mary's Hospital, the largest clinic in the city, a heavy atmosphere prevailed, marked by despair and exhaustion. In the overcrowded corridors, tired sighs and snippets of hushed conversations could be heard. Patients with oxygen masks sat apathetically on the cool tiles, their eyes empty and full of resignation. Others lay coughing on stretchers while their relatives desperately sought help.

Dr. Ruth White, an experienced pulmonologist, was gripped by an inner restlessness as she began her shift. Flipping through patient files, the feeling of helplessness intensified with each entry. "The number of severe cases of bronchitis and acute asthma attacks is skyrocketing," she said to Dr. Eric Miller, a young resident whose wide eyes betrayed how overwhelmed he felt.

"What should we do?" Eric asked hesitantly.

"Our top priority is to provide patients with enough oxygen and prevent life-threatening complications. It's no longer just affecting the weakest—it can hit anyone now."

Suddenly, a nurse hurried toward them, her face etched with exhaustion and worry. "Dr. White, there are no more free beds. How should we proceed?" Her voice trembled slightly.

"Set up additional makeshift beds in the cafeteria and waiting areas," the pulmonologist replied. "Use everything we have—blankets, pillows, mats. We must not turn anyone away."

As Dr. White and the young doctor rushed through the overcrowded corridors, they came upon a young mother desperately cradling her wheezing child. The mother was pale, her eyes red from crying, despair written all over her face. Dr. White felt her heart tighten. In her distress, the young mother grabbed Eric's arm, tears in her eyes. "Please, help her!"

Eric, his face reddened from hours of wearing the protective mask, kneeled beside the child. The girl's red coat rose and fell irregularly as she shook uncontrollably. He listened to the rattling breath with his stethoscope. Panic rose within him at her worsening condition; his hands began to shake, sweat ran down his forehead into his eyes. He blinked and looked into the pleading eyes of the mother. The deep despair on her face constricted his throat; her trembling lips formed words he could not hear. The responsibility weighed heavily on his shoulders. Suddenly, the air in the room seemed thicker, heavier.

"We're doing everything we can!" he finally burst out, his voice rough and tense. "But...," his throat tightened further. "It's just not enough!" With a helpless gesture, he pointed to the overcrowded corridor. "We don't have enough resources—too many patients... too few hands to help everyone!"

His words echoed through the corridor. A tense silence settled over the exhausted people, who suddenly all listened.

Dr. White calmly stepped beside him, placing a firm hand on his shoulder. "Eric," she said with gentle emphasis. "I know how hard this is. We all feel the pressure, but we must stay strong—for the patients and for ourselves." She squeezed his shoulder lightly and pulled him aside. "Go outside. Take a deep breath. You need a break. I'll take over here."

The clinic was operating at its limit; makeshift solutions had become the norm. The exhausted staff didn't know how much longer they could hold out. Each new patient brought additional challenges, and Dr. White felt the constant pressure of making decisions that determined life and death. She thought back to a time when she knew each patient personally and had enough time for everyone. Now she felt like a small cog in an overloaded system.

As she paused for a moment and looked out the window, she noticed the dense haze enveloping the city. The oppressive reality hit her with full force. *How are people out there surviving this?*

Beyond the hospital walls, the city lay frozen under a heavy fog slowly suffocating it. The biting smell of burnt coal hung in the air, and despite protective masks, smog seeped into the airways of the few people who ventured outside. Their faces were hidden behind filters, their eyes filled with concern. The few passersby hastily ran their errands and quickly fled back to their homes. Their frightened glances reflected a silent panic that spread inexorably through the streets.

By now, the city resembled an apocalyptic scene where the air had become a bitter enemy. Indiscriminate in who it targeted, it fueled an omnipresent fear for all. Each new death deepened the collective feeling of grief and helplessness in Plainfield. The crematoriums worked tirelessly—a constant reminder of the threat.

Although the government was alarmed, real solutions were lacking. People felt abandoned, trapped in a world that was robbing them of breath. The education system also suffered under the growing emergency.

Ian Becker let out a deep sigh. *Three more students absent...* Of his 26 students, only seven were online today. The few children who had logged in sat focused in front of their screens, engrossed in the exercise. *How are we supposed to maintain any semblance of normality?* The constant absences led to growing gaps in knowledge that even dedicated teachers could no longer close. Becker could recall the lively chatter in the classroom, the heated discussions, the restrained giggling from the back rows. Suddenly, the memory of the day when the principal had announced, "Everyone go home. Classes will be held online from now on," surfaced. Back then, Ian had believed it was only a temporary measure, a pause in the midst of the crisis. Years had passed since, and a return to normalcy seemed more distant than ever. Shaking his head, he uploaded the homework to the school's network.

"Mr. Becker, I'm done with the assignments," a student reported over the microphone.

"Well done, Anna," he responded. "Does anyone else have questions?" Silence. No screen showed any reaction. He sighed again and ended the class. *The children need support that I can't give them.*

That evening, after another frustrating day, he spoke with his wife. "Many students are absent because they're sick or have to help at home. And many of those who want to participate struggle with technical problems."

"I can see how much this burdens you," she replied gently. "Don't forget how important you are to the children. You give them stability."

Ian sighed deeply. "Sometimes I wonder if it even makes a difference. It's getting worse," he replied with a bitter undertone. "Wealthier families can afford to hire a personal tutor, but disadvantaged households... they hardly stand a chance. Education is increasingly becoming a privilege, and the gap between social classes keeps growing."

His wife placed her hand on his knee. "I know it's hard, but what you're doing has great value. For some children, you might be the only ray of hope."

He thought of the students who, despite everything, hadn't given up on their education. *Maybe... maybe there is hope after all.*

In one of the few cafés still open, Marlene, an elderly lady with carefully styled gray hair, sat alone at a table. Her clouded eyes stared through the window into the fog as she thought about the rapid transformation of her beloved city. This café had once been a regular meeting place for her and her friends. One of them, always healthy and full of energy, had suddenly passed away two weeks earlier. The empty chair across from her now seemed like a silent witness to the loss. In her heart, Marlene knew that the Gray Winter was to blame. Her other friends had barricaded themselves in their homes, windows tightly closed as if death lurked outside.

Marlene felt alone and abandoned. The shared hours in the café had been her anchor. Now everything seemed gray and meaningless. The soft murmur from the radio reached her ears. She didn't understand every word. One kept repeating: *Violet.*

They hadn't moved their weekly meetings online. For Marlene and her friends, personal togetherness was irreplaceable. The laughter, the lively conversations—*online lacks warmth.* Yet she came here every week, determined to hold on to something of her formal life.

Again, she heard the word *violet* from the radio, accompanied by a dramatic voice emphasizing the acute threat. Marlene sighed and leaned back. She found herself saying aloud, "Sometimes I wonder if those in charge are really doing everything to tackle this crisis. Why did it have to come to this? Are there plans we don't know about?" Her eyes met those of the barista. His forehead was deeply lined with concern. "I just hope they find a solution soon, before it's too late," she said to him. "Not for us old folks, but for the young ones who deserve a future—a future brighter and more livable than this endless gray nightmare."

The barista slowly walked over to the old radio in the corner and turned it off. Then he sat down with her. They spoke softly about the latest news, rumors of technological breakthroughs, and a faint hope that the situation wouldn't worsen further.

It was the middle of the night when Hannah Kowalski was still sitting over the petri dishes in the lab. In front of her were the thawed biofilms, which she had treated with the utmost precision, according to the instructions in her lab notebook. Every step had been carried out meticulously, just like with the highly efficient biofilms that had previously been destroyed in the reactor. Despite her care, she couldn't be sure whether these cells would eliminate the pollutants as successfully as they had. Microorganisms didn't adhere to mathematical rules—they were alive, unpredictable.

Part of her knew that after the last flare-up of her MS, she should have slowed down. The high-dose cortisone therapy had been several weeks ago, and fortunately, the symptoms had subsided well. Permanent damage seemed unlikely. Dr. Kramer had advised her to avoid stress to prevent a relapse, but Hannah was determined to complete this test before going home. *Just this one result, then I'll finally take a break.*

Deep inside, guilt gnawed at her. *If I hadn't been out of action for weeks because of my MS, I might have been able to work on the biofilms earlier and prevent the escalation of the Gray Winter.* This thought weighed so heavily on her shoulders that it felt as if it was pressing her down.

Anxiously, Hannah waited for the test result of the pollutant absorption. Nervously, she drummed her fingers on the table before admonishing herself to calm down. *Stop, that doesn't help. Stay calm.* She forced herself to lay her hands flat on the lab table, feeling its cold metal, and tried to take deep breaths, but her gaze inevitably wandered back to the screen, as if doing so could make the result appear faster. *Come on, already!*

Finally, the result flashed on the screen—negative. The biofilm was largely ineffective against the pollutants. A cry of frustration escaped her, echoing throughout the empty lab. Her hands clenched into fists; her fingernails dug painfully into her palms. For a moment, she stared in disbelief at the result. Disappointment paralyzed her. But she eventually pulled herself together. A solution was needed now; time was relentlessly working against her.

CHAPTER 10
ROBERT BENNET –
THE TURNING POINT

In the dark hours of the night, as the hospital room was enveloped in an ominous silence, Bennet kept vigil at the bedside of his granddaughter. The monotonous sounds of the life-support machines were the only constants in this oppressive quiet. Ella, only eight years old, suffered from severe asthma exacerbated by the relentless air pollution. Battling for breath each night, Bennet hoped that his presence provided her at least some comfort. Since the situation in Plainfield had deteriorated, his worry for Ella had only grown.

Bennet had intended to go home once Ella was sleeping soundly, but an inner restlessness—a nagging feeling of concern—kept him at her bedside. In the dim light of the room, and as the machines emitted their soothing hum, memories of her fifth birthday surfaced in his mind. They had spent a sunny afternoon in the park, experiencing the warmth and delight only a child can radiate. Ella, in a light blue dress adorned with small butterflies, had stood proudly before her homemade piñata, surrounded by friends and family eagerly awaiting the moment the candies would spill out. Bennet recalled how Ella had looked at him with big, shining eyes and asked if butterflies knew how happy they made the world. He had laughed and assured her that she herself spread more joy than all the butterflies combined ever could.

That simple, happy day stood in stark contrast to the present reality. The park where they had celebrated was now overgrown with weeds, the air too toxic for children's games, and the world Ella lived in had become different—one that barely gave her room to breathe. Bennet's heart ached at the thought that such carefree days might forever belong to the past.

A shrill beeping tore him from his thoughts—all the devices in the room sounded an alarm. Bennet flinched in shock. Seconds later, the lights went out, and a paralyzing darkness spread, accompanied by an eerie silence. A power outage? Bennet's pulse raced as he desperately waited for the emergency power to kick in. Nothing happened. The machines remained silent.

Panic seized the hospital; loud shouts and hurried footsteps echoed through the corridors. The smell of disinfectants mingled with rising fear. Ella, awakened by the abrupt beeping, began desperately gasping for air. Her small hand slipped from Bennet's grasp as she flailed her arms in panic. "Ella!" he called out, his voice breaking. In the total darkness, Bennet fumbled for his mobile phone, his fingers trembling. Finally, he activated the flashlight function. The sparse light cast eerie shadows on Ella's face, her eyes wide with panic. She couldn't breathe anymore.

Desperately, Bennet searched for a manual oxygen pump. He yanked open drawers, rummaged through cabinets, but found nothing. His hands shook uncontrollably; cold sweat stood on his forehead. He pressed the emergency button next to the bed, but nothing happened. "Help! Please, someone help!" he shouted into the hallway, but his pleas were lost in the tumult. He grasped Ella's hand again, squeezing it tightly. "I'm here with you. I won't leave you alone," he whispered, his voice quavering with fear.

In the hospital corridor, pure chaos reigned; the darkness swallowed everything. People collided, screams and sobbing filled the hallways. Bennet occasionally saw flashlight beams hastily passing by as the staff feverishly tried to calm patients. The desperate cries of doctors and nurses mingled with the hysteria of the patients. Ella's breathing became increasingly shallow; her small body trembled.

Minutes stretched like hours, and every second without oxygen dramatically worsened her condition. *What should I do?* Bennet felt torn between the urge to get help and the fear of leaving Ella alone. In panicked desperation, he decided to act. He placed his mouth over hers and hastily blew air into her lungs. "Breathe, Ella, please breathe!" he begged, tears streaming down his face.

When the doctors finally burst into the room, illuminating the space with flashlights, they acted immediately, their faces marked by worry and tension. "We'll take over now," one said quietly to Bennet, but he couldn't let go of Ella.

They placed a manual ventilation mask on her and began resuscitation. With routine yet desperate movements, they performed chest compressions, pumping oxygen into her tiny lungs. The mechanical clicking of the ventilation mask and the strained breathing of the doctors filled the room, while the weak light of the flashlights cast ghostly shadows on the walls. Bennet watched as they fought for her life. His heart clenched with every breath.

"Please, Ella, hold on," he whispered, tears running uncontrollably down his face. For several agonizing minutes, the medical team did everything to bring Ella back, but her being without oxygen had already taken its toll. Slowly, the intensity waned; their movements became more sluggish, hope gave way to resignation.

Eventually, they had to cease their efforts. The lead doctor removed the manual oxygen mask, his expression empty, exhausted. With his head bowed, he approached Bennet, who was still clutching Ella's cold hand. "We are deeply sorry, Mr. Bennet," the doctor said softly, his voice filled with compassion. "We did everything we could. She is... it's too late."

It was as if Bennet's heart had been torn from his chest. The restless flickering of the flashlights, the hectic whispering of the doctors in the background—all of it faded away. After a moment of deep silence, the doctor placed a hand on Bennet's shoulder, then turned to tend to the next desperate patient.

Bennet remained alone. Stunned, he stared down at Ella, her face now peaceful but without the glow that once filled it. Something irretrievably broke within him. Beams of light streaming in from the corridor cast dancing shadows over her, as if they wanted to let Ella's life flare up one last time.

Slowly, his legs buckled, and he sank to his knees beside her bed. With trembling hands, he pulled Ella's lifeless body close, holding her tight as if that might bring her back to life. "No, no, no..." he whispered over and over, his voice barely more than a hoarse prayer. Immeasurable grief and helplessness overwhelmed him; tears streamed endlessly down his face.

The realization that he had been powerless in those crucial moments tore him apart inside. In that instant, time seemed to stand still; Bennet felt nothing but the piercing pain of loss that overshadowed everything else. The world around him blurred, became meaningless. There was only him and Ella, frozen in a moment he would never forget.

As the first timid signs of dawn filtered through the windows, the harsh hospital lights suddenly flickered back on, snapping Bennet out of his stupor. For a moment, he irrationally hoped that Ella would return too, that life would flow back into her with the light. But as his gaze fell upon her lifeless body, reality hit him once more with full force.

Exhausted, he let himself fall onto the nearest chair. His legs shook from kneeling for so long, and it felt as if they had lost all strength to support him. *How am I supposed to go on without her?* A deep sense of emptiness spread within him, as if someone had torn a hole in his innermost being. *What meaning does my life have without my beloved Ella?* This paralyzing question gnawed at him. He found no answer.

Tears burned in his eyes, but alongside the immeasurable grief, something else stirred. A glowing anger began to smolder within him—anger at a world that allowed such a tragedy, at a society that stood idly by while children like Ella had to suffer. *How has it come to this?* His heart pounded fiercely; his thoughts spiraled. *Science has failed, the government looked away. They have all abandoned us.*

"Why?" he whispered into the silence, his voice breaking under the weight of his emotions. "Why doesn't anyone do something?" The questions echoed in his head, unanswered and tormenting. With trembling hands, he wiped the tears from his eyes and slowly stood up.

It was time to go home, but what did home mean now? Without Ella, everything seemed pointless. On the way back through the empty streets, which looked desolate in the pale morning light, he reached for his mobile phone. His fingers shook as he dialed Judith's number to deliver the terrible news to his daughter. The pain was overwhelming, a heavy burden weighing on his shoulders and nearly crushing him. Deep inside, the determined rage continued to boil, crying out for retribution.

CHAPTER 11
YOUNG ADULTS –
THROUGH THE VIOLET FOG

Several weeks after their departure from Plainfield, the situation had dramatically worsened for Alex, Lara, and the other young people. The environmental monitor showed continuous purple—a clear signal of increasing danger.

They pushed further south, passing by largely deserted cities and villages. The facades of the houses were covered with soot and fine dust that lay like a suffocating blanket over everything. An eerie silence hung everywhere, interrupted only by the rustling of the wind sweeping through the abandoned alleys. The smell of burned material penetrated through their breathing masks, causing them to grimace.

The only signs of life were faint flickering lights behind some windows—voiceless witnesses of the isolated souls enduring this desolation.

Needing to stop frequently to change their breathing masks, the toxins were affecting the group more than they had expected, and Basil was increasingly struggling with a dry cough that worried them all. "I can handle it," he tried to assure them, but his pale skin told a different story.

Procuring food presented another challenge that required thoughtful planning. In the few supermarkets still open, they made sure to buy long-lasting packets and cans, as they could never be certain when they would come across another open store.

Every day was a battle. The bicycles, their most important companions, demanded regular maintenance. Alex often kneeled by the roadside to fix flat tires or repair a jammed chain. The dense fog surrounding them barely allowed them to see their hands in front of their faces, forcing them to drastically reduce their speed. Potholes and deep cracks in the roads became dangerous traps obscured by the smog.

"The air quality here is catastrophic," Naomi said one morning as they discussed the day's route.

"We can take a detour," Tom suggested, visibly struggling to keep his composure. "It would take longer, but we'd be safer."

The tension was palpable. Every breath they took through their masks felt heavier. Fatigue and uncertainty weighed on them, and the constant pressure of the poor air quality made them doubt the feasibility of their endeavor. Basil coughed again, this time more severely. Tom looked at him with a worried frown. "We need a break," he finally said.

Every evening, they desperately searched for a safe refuge before darkness fully set in. Usually, they were lucky enough to find shelter with hospitable locals, who offered them not only a place to sleep but also a warm meal and something to drink, invaluable in these uncertain times. On nights when they didn't find hospitality, they sought refuge in abandoned barns or empty school buildings. These places were often dusty and deserted but offered at least minimal barriers against the toxic environment. On such nights, they wore their masks throughout, increasing the strain and dampening their spirits.

Despite all adversity, they stuck together. Naomi tried to lift the mood by telling stories or singing. Basil, though weakened, joked about the improvised menus made from various canned goods. But reality kept catching up with them, and the question of whether they would reach their goal hung over them like a dark shadow.

As they gathered that night in a classroom, they were met with the stench of decay. Despite the masks, they could smell the rotting wood and damp plaster. Old pictures painted by students from happier days still hung on the walls, reminding them of a long-gone, unattainable time.

Naomi sat on a dusty school bench, scrolling through the comments on their latest video. "Hey guys, look at this," she said with a weak smile. "*You are our eyes and ears out there. Stay strong; we are praying for you.*"

She looked up, her eyes searching the room for reactions. Alex leaned against the wall and let out a short, bitter laugh. "Great, eyes and ears... would be cool if they could be our lungs instead." The sarcasm in his voice couldn't entirely mask the reassurance the comment gave him.

Naomi swallowed hard as she read more of the comments. "They're really pinning all their hopes on us," she murmured. "*I have asthma and follow each of your videos. I hope each time that you've finally found a place where the air is better. Please don't give up, you're my last hope.*"

Tears welled up in Naomi's eyes, and the responsibility weighing on all of them suddenly felt overwhelming. In the oppressive silence, they heard the distant dripping of water and the occasional rustling of small animals nesting in the ruins of the school building.

Tom closed his eyes, letting the words sink in. "Wow," he finally murmured. "Our videos are like a glimmer of hope for them."

Alex stared at the floor, his fists deep in his pockets. "And every time we post something new, it's another disappointment. Still no clean place... everything's messed up, as usual." An old knot formed in his stomach. *What if there really is no better place?* He pushed the thought away, recalling his father's last words: "If you don't like it here, then go. Find a place where you can live." *I can't return empty-handed. Then I've failed.*

Lara's breath caught. She jumped up, her mobile phone in hand, eyes widened. "This can't be true!" she exclaimed with a trembling voice. "Guys, the video from SouthHope... it's gone!"

The others looked at her, confused.

"What do you mean, gone?" Naomi asked.

"They deleted it," Lara explained, her voice quavering. "They say it was fake."

Naomi gasped. "Seriously? That's why we left home! And now it's all just a fake?"

Tom rubbed his forehead, looking tiredly around the group. "I suspected it... Everywhere we've passed through has looked terrible, nothing like in the video. We're risking our lives for a lie." He regarded each of them seriously. "Let's turn back before it's too late... before we end up dying out here." His eyes desperately sought agreement as his fingers nervously drummed on his knees. "Every day, breathing gets harder, and our masks won't last much longer. Maybe the south isn't the paradise we're hoping for, but just another dead end."

The air in the room seemed even heavier. A faint creaking sounded in the hallway as the wind swept through the silent corridors of the school building. Alex jumped up, his face tense with anger. "Are you kidding me, Tom? Do you really want to chicken out now?" His voice quivered with rage. "Okay, the video was fake, but everyone knows the air is better in the south. If you want to give up now, then go back and hide! But I'm not giving up. There has to be somewhere better."

"Stop this nonsense!" Lara said urgently, her voice trembling slightly with anger. "We have to stick together. If we start fighting now, we're done for."

Tom stood up as well, his eyes flashing with suppressed anger. "It's not about giving up!" he shouted back. "It's about whether this all still makes sense! Look at us—we're totally exhausted. Some of us can barely breathe!" He pointed at Basil, whose pale face spoke volumes.

Basil nodded weakly. "It's true, I can hardly breathe anymore. We really need to be careful."

Alex stepped toward Tom, his voice turning cold. "Then just leave if that's how you feel. I'm going to keep fighting. We can't bury our heads in the sand every time things get tough."

Tom clenched his fists, nearly shouting now. "It's not about cowardice, man! It's about our lives! What's the point if we die here before we even reach the south?"

Alex took another step toward Tom, their faces inches apart. "Do you even hear yourself?" he snarled.

Then things escalated quickly. Before the others could intervene, Alex grabbed Tom by the collar. "You want to throw everything away?" he shouted. Tom broke free and shoved Alex so hard that he stumbled against an old, wobbly desk. The desk tipped over; Alex lost his balance and crashed to the floor. Heart racing, Alex clenched his hands into fists so tightly that his knuckles turned white. Tom felt adrenaline coursing through his veins, and his nostrils flared with each breath.

Alex got back up and charged at Tom. Both staggered and fell to the ground, throwing punches at each other. The rest of the group recoiled in shock.

For a moment, Naomi, Lara, and Basil stood rooted to the spot. Then Naomi rushed forward, closely followed by the others. They forced themselves between the fighters, trying to separate them.

"That's enough!" Basil shouted before his voice was choked by a coughing fit.

Clear but desperate, Naomi made herself heard: "Stop! This isn't getting us anywhere!"

Lara pulled Alex back. "Please, Alex, let it go. We have to stick together."

Despite all efforts, the atmosphere in the room remained tense. The youths withdrew into themselves, each absorbed in their own thoughts. Tom sat apart, staring silently into the darkness, while Alex, still trembling with anger, had retreated to the other end of the room. Naomi stared thoughtfully at the ceiling. *We must not fall apart. We are all we have left.*

The night brought little sleep; uncertainty and the weight of an unresolved decision kept them awake. The wind outside and the occasional creaking of the building intensified the feeling of hopelessness.

The next morning, the mood was still subdued. As they

packed their things, Alex and Tom avoided eye contact. Lara decided to initiate a conversation. "Hey, can we talk for a moment?" she asked quietly to the group. "We can't go on like this."

Tom sighed, looking at the ground. "Maybe I overreacted," he admitted. "I just don't want anyone to get hurt."

Alex gave him a brief glance. "We're all at our limit," he said. "But we can't give up."

Naomi stepped up to them. "We have to stick together, no matter how hard it gets."

A brief smile flitted across Tom's face. "Okay," he said. "Together, we can do it."

They continued their journey on a path through a dense forest. The youths felt as if they were entering another world. One where green trees grew and birdsong could be heard—sights and sounds they had missed for a long time. Their hearts felt lighter as they inhaled the fresh scent of earth and plants, a welcome contrast to the suffocating smog they were used to. A delicate smile played on their lips, but a slight melancholy reflected in their eyes, as if they sensed the fleetingness of this moment.

The forest, a temporary refuge, seemed to dissolve the tensions among them. Naomi, passionate about botany, led the others on foot along a narrow path deeper into the woods. Suddenly, Alex stopped and excitedly pointed to a spot at the edge of a clearing. "Look!"

They all followed his gaze and held their breath. Before them lay a group of bright blue cornflowers, their intense color vividly contrasting against the green backdrop. The flowers seemed to sparkle like little jewels in the sun.

Naomi jumped with joy. "They're incredibly beautiful!" she exclaimed. She hurried to the flowers and knelt down to examine them more closely, her eyes sparkling with excitement. "You know," she began eagerly, "my grandma used to tell me stories about cornflowers. She said they were a sign that life finds its way even in the harshest environments."

Basil cautiously stepped closer, reaching out to touch the

cornflowers gently with his fingertips. "Are they really real?" he asked incredulously.

Tom grinned, shaking his head. "Yes, Basil, they're real. Not a hologram or anything."

Basil laughed bitterly. "After all that gray, I almost forgot what real colors look like."

Alex nodded in agreement. "I know exactly what you mean. It almost feels surreal."

The unexpected beauty of nature gave Tom new resolve. "It's like a gift. Maybe there are other places like this," he said thoughtfully, "places where life prevails." He straightened up, his eyes expressing new determination. "We have a responsibility to find them and perhaps even protect them. That gives our journey a deeper meaning." Alex patted Tom on the shoulder, nodding happily that they shared a common goal again.

A feeling of unity flowed through them. "Maybe we're like these cornflowers," Lara said with a smile. "Despite everything, we're still standing."

In this hopeful moment, they spontaneously decided to hold a small ceremony. The youths stood in a circle, their hands gently clasped over the glowing cornflowers.

"Let's make a promise," Naomi said firmly. "Come what may, we won't give up. Not just for ourselves, but for all living things—for every flower, every bird, every tree."

They closed their eyes, feeling the warm touch of their friends' hands. "We are more than just wanderers. We are ambassadors of hope," Tom declared confidently.

As they parted from one another, the air seemed lighter, as if an invisible weight had been lifted from their shoulders. Every step they took from then on was carried by a deep understanding of their role in tackling this great challenge.

Before continuing their journey, they decided to share this special place with their followers, showing them the symbol of hope that the cornflowers represented. Lara pulled out her smartphone and began filming the scene.

Naomi looked into the camera and spoke softly: "These flowers are proof that life can thrive even under the harshest conditions. They are a sign of hope for all of us." The video, filled with their thoughts on the journey and environmental protection, was then uploaded on their social networks.

As they continued their journey, they fixed their gaze firmly on the goal: to find a place where they could breathe freely without fear.

CHAPTER 12
MARCUS LEONARD –
THE FAILED ENVIRONMENTAL LAW AND
THE LEONARD EFFECT

Ten years ago, in 2037, the environmental crisis had reached a critical peak. Cities were suffocating in smog, waters were poisoned, and people suffered from the consequences. The Global Protocol for Clean Air (GPCA) emerged as an urgent response, aiming to introduce strict emission limits, intensify the use of renewable energies, and greatly restrict the use of harmful substances. There was considerable hope that this law could initiate a worldwide shift towards a more sustainable future.

Marcus Leonard stood at the edge of a conference room in the New York State Assembly. His eyes wandered over the faces of the politicians and business leaders present. Outside, beyond the tall windows, thick clouds hung over the city, and the sun struggled in vain to send its light through the dense veil. In some countries, the protocol had already been tentatively ratified, and the first positive effects on the environment were evident. Now it was time to implement the measures worldwide.

Leonard's gaze lingered on a group of business leaders gathered in a corner of the hall. Among them was a woman in a gray suit, the CEO of a large technology company. She looked thoughtful and was in quiet discussion with a stout man, the head of a multinational industrial corporation. "The GPCA will bring our industry to its knees," said the man, his face flushed. "Our production costs will explode. If we have to comply with these limits, we'll be forced to close locations. Jobs will be destroyed, families will suffer."

The woman in the suit replied calmly, "I understand your concerns, but we also have to consider the long-term consequences. A sick environment ultimately harms the economy as well. Maybe we can promote investments in green technologies and thus achieve both goals."

The man shook his head. "That all sounds well and good, but our shareholders expect profits, not risky endeavors."

Leonard felt a heaviness spreading in his chest. He understood the worries of both sides. The faces of the men and women in the corner were marked by anger—a dark premonition of what Plainfield might face.

Back at his workplace in Plainfield, Leonard sat in the dimmed conference room of the town hall, surrounded by the city's most influential industrialists. The atmosphere was tense. With a barely touched cup of coffee before him, he listened to the heated discussions.

Mr. Miller, owner of a traditional mechanical engineering company, leaned forward. His words carried the weight of an ultimatum. "Marcus, if the law passes, we'll move our production abroad. That would mean mass layoffs. The city would bleed."

Ms. Bailey, head of a medium-sized chemical company, sitting on the other side of the room, added, "Our research is already establishing more environmentally friendly processes, but we can't switch everything overnight. If the law passes in its current form, we'll have to shut down."

Leonard remained silent, but his thoughts raced feverishly. He envisioned hordes of unemployed people, exploding social costs, factories becoming ruins, broken families... The decision seemed clear: the GPCA could not be implemented in Plainfield. There had to be another way—one that protected the economy and saved the city from collapse.

Only days later, Mikael, a passionate environmental activist, stood in the parliamentary hall. His heart pounded with excitement. Beside him, a like-minded politician nodded in agreement as Mikael spoke firmly: "The Global Protocol for Clean Air is our chance for a livable future," he called out to the deputies, holding up the master document of the GPCA.

"Imagine if our children could breathe clean air, in a world where nature and humans live in harmony. If we don't act now, when will we? If not us, who else? Do we really want to watch as greed and convenience destroy the Earth?" His voice grew more urgent, the passion in his words palpable. "It's time to have the courage to take responsibility. Not tomorrow, not next week— now! The world is watching us. The decisions we make today determine the course for future generations."

He paused briefly to regard the audience. "Let's make history together. Let's show that we not only talk but also act. For clean air, for a healthy Earth, and for the future of our children!"

The expressions of the deputies suggested agreement, but in the dark corners of the parliamentary corridors, the lobbyists of the fossil fuel industry had already done their work, striving to enforce their interests. Dressed in expensive suits, they had whispered promises and threats to the politicians, placing many deputies in a quandary.

Shortly before the decisive vote, they gathered for a final debate. The atmosphere was charged as Marcus Leonard stepped up to the podium. His voice was calm, his eyes reflecting the seriousness of the situation. "Ladies and gentlemen, the GPCA is a well-intentioned proposal. The goals associated with it are close to my heart," he began. "But we must consider the reality of our national economy, which is the lifeline of our country. We all strive for a clean environment, but many companies face enormous challenges. If we implement the GPCA in its current form, we risk not only the loss of thousands of jobs, we will also be jeopardizing social peace."

He let his gaze sweep through the hall. "Plainfield's prosperity is based on a stable economic environment. We must not jeopardize it through hasty measures. Instead, we should choose a more balanced approach that secures both environmental protection and our economic future. I therefore ask you to vote against the GPCA today and instead support an approach that does not lead our country into an uncertain future."

Immediately, murmurs spread through the rows of delegates. Some deputies nodded in agreement; others exchanged worried glances.

Mikael jumped up, his frustration evident. "What good is a strong economy if we destroy our very means of living?" he declared passionately. His words echoed through the hall as the deputies looked between Leonard and Mikael in uncertainty.

When it came to the vote, a narrow majority followed Leonard's argument and voted against the GPCA. Horror and deep disappointment were reflected in the faces of its supporters. Mikael clenched his fist under the table; his dream of a groundbreaking environmental protection law that would improve air quality and protect future generations had been shattered.

Outside the parliament, environmental activists, concerned citizens, and families with children had gathered. Their eyes were fixed on the screens broadcasting the parliamentary debate live. Hope and concern hung in the air. When the result was announced, a collective groan of disappointment went through the crowd.

On social media, heated discussions ignited immediately. *How could they?* and *Our future was just sold!* read the comment sections. The hashtag *#LeonardEffect* went viral and became a symbol of the anger and disappointment. It henceforth stood for the prioritization of economic interests over ecological sustainability.

In the following weeks, environmental conditions continued to deteriorate. Thick smog lay over the cities; the number of respiratory diseases rose rapidly. Hospitals were overcrowded, and doctors warned of the health consequences of air pollution.

Leonard sat late at night in his office, the news playing on his computer. Images of protesting people, polluted rivers, and dying forests flickered across the screen. A feeling of unease crept over him, but he pushed it aside. *We are working on a solution. It just requires patience.*

Over time, as environmental conditions became unbearable, the term Gray Winter established itself to describe the grim reality in which people now lived. Criticism of the parliament's decision steadily grew. The rejection of the GPCA was repeatedly cited as a crucial mistake that could have been avoided.

CHAPTER 13
ROBERT BENNET –
THE PATH OF REVENGE

In the days following Ella's death, Bennet's heart was enveloped in deep darkness. Driven by pain and anger, he sought an outlet. He came across reports of Mikael's courageous protest against the government's inaction. The images of Mikael, with a raised fist and angry gaze, gave Bennet a direction for his rage—against those responsible for the entire disaster. Consumed by his desire for revenge, he typed an anonymous message on Mikael's website: *Who do you believe bears the greatest blame for the government's failure that led to the Gray Winter?*

Bennet spent a restless night. Unable to sleep, he paced his apartment like a caged animal. He refreshed the webpage repeatedly until his eyes burned. Finally, as the first morning light pierced through the windows and chased away the shadows, a reply arrived. *Marcus Leonard blocked the GPCA, on which I and other environmental organizations had worked for years. His decisions led to an escalation of the environmental crisis—see Leonard Effect.*

With this information, Bennet finally had a clear enemy in sight. He delved deeper into his research and soon discovered the address of Leonard, who was now a city councilor. Driven by his new goal, he set out one evening with a pistol he had once acquired for home protection, intending to hold Leonard accountable.

Bennet took the subway to the suburbs and then walked to a wealthy area that seemed almost isolated from the outside world. His heart pounded in his chest as he stood before the large iron gate, behind which Leonard's estate stretched. In front of him was an intercom. He took a deep breath, pressed the bell, and waited while sweat beaded on his forehead. A tired-sounding female voice finally spoke: "Can I help you?"

"Good evening, my name is Robert Bennet. I urgently need to speak in person with Dr. Leonard. It's about a previous collaboration in environmental protection," Bennet lied, his voice firm while attempting to sound friendly.

After a short pause, the gate buzzed and slowly opened. Bennet's heart beat even faster. His lie had been plausible enough to grant him entry.

Bennet had prepared himself to confront an aloof politician, but instead, Claudia Leonard, the councilor's wife, appeared at the door, leaning weakly against it. Her shoulders hung slack as she gasped for air; her body appeared emaciated and weak. Despite the visible effort each movement cost her, she greeted Bennet with a friendly smile, her warmth seeming to overshadow her obvious pain. "We seldom receive visitors these days," she said with shining eyes that revealed her joy at the unexpected guest. "Would you like something to drink or perhaps a piece of cake?"

Bennet, suddenly aware of his original, sinister intention, cleared his throat. "No, thank you," he said curtly. The unexpected kindness of the woman made him uncertain. Not knowing what to do with his hands, he finally stuck them in his coat pockets, where he felt the pistol. His stomach tightened unpleasantly. He avoided looking her in the eyes.

Claudia coughed laboriously as she led Bennet inside, her hand resting protectively on her evidently aching chest. Slowly, she sat down at the table and put on a mask connected to a portable oxygen tank. Her struggle painfully reminded Bennet of

Ella. His hand, which had been gripping the pistol, began to relax. Doubts about his plan rose within him. Bennet closed his eyes. *What am I actually doing here?* The memory of Ella's laughter mingled with the sight of Claudia's suffering. In the silence of his inner turmoil, he felt the weight of the pistol in his pocket. It suddenly seemed unbearably heavy. His fingers shook slightly as he slowly gripped and then released the weapon. Taking a deep breath, he felt a wave of shame and doubt wash over him. *Can I really kill a person?* His heart pounded in his chest, as if trying to bring him to his senses.

"I have to rest after a few steps because I suffer from advanced COPD," Claudia explained with a weak smile as she adjusted the mask. "Every breath is a reminder of what we've lost. Marcus is doing his best to make a difference, but politics is a murky water," she added pensively.

"I watched my granddaughter suffer day after day, and nothing could ease her pain," Bennet said, his voice trembling slightly. "That pain remains and keeps dragging me back into the abyss."

Claudia nodded, her eyes full of compassion. "It's hard to live with this pain each day. Every time I turn on my oxygen tank, I wonder how many breaths we have left." She paused briefly before continuing. "In my condition, I can't do much anymore. That's why I hope and pray that everything will soon turn for the better." Her gaze met his. In their pain, they were connected.

At that moment, she appeared to remember the reason for Bennet's visit. "My husband is upstairs. He works like a man possessed, day and night, to improve the situation. I'll call him." She made a move to get up again, but Bennet raised his hand reassuringly.

"No, please, don't trouble yourself," he said gently, his voice now carrying an unexpected softness. "It's not as urgent as I thought." Claudia's kind words and her visible inner struggle had deeply moved him and caused him to pause. He realized that revenge would only bring more suffering. Perhaps the true path to justice lay in forgiveness and striving for change, not in retribution. "I should go," he murmured.

Claudia hesitated, visibly confused by the sudden change in his tone. "Are you sure?" she asked, her tone filled with concern and a hint of mistrust.

"Yes, I'm sure," Bennet replied, his voice tinged with quiet melancholy. "Thank you for your hospitality."

Bennet turned and walked hurriedly to the front door. As he left the house, he felt Claudia's puzzled gaze on his back. The heavy burden of revenge that had led him to this house began to dissolve, replaced by a deeper, painful understanding of shared human suffering that knew no boundaries.

With each step away from the house, Bennet felt his perspective on the world shifting. The personal struggles and silent suffering, even in this affluent environment, reminded him that the problems he faced went far beyond individual or simple political solutions.

On the way home, Bennet felt a mixture of relief and deep sorrow. The pressure of the planned retribution that had darkened his thoughts was gone, but the gravity of the situation and the universal nature of suffering weighed heavily on him. As he walked through the quiet, foggy streets, he thought of his encounter with Claudia, who, despite her own health problems, maintained dignity and compassion. He also thought of Ella, and of the futility of hate and violence.

At home, Bennet found his wife, Martha, in the living room, where she had been anxiously awaiting his return. Revealing his visit to the Leonards and what he had planned, he told of the sobering realization that the family of the man he had wanted to hold accountable for Ella's death had also experienced the devastating consequences of the environmental crisis. "I just couldn't do it," he confessed to his wife. "It wouldn't have changed anything for the better. They're suffering just like we are."

Martha placed a hand on his cheek. "We've both lost so much," she whispered. "Maybe we can find a new beginning together, instead of dwelling in anger and revenge."

Bennet nodded, comforted by Martha's closeness. The exhaustion that overcame him felt relieving, as if a heavy burden had been lifted. That night, Bennet lay to rest his dark plan, and took a decisive step toward healing.

CHAPTER 14
MARCUS LEONARD –
A POLITICIAN AT A CROSSROADS

Dr. Marcus Leonard stood at the window of his study, staring out at the once radiant gardens now smothered by a dull, opaque veil of smog. He used to find peace and tranquility in this greenery, but the dense haze had swallowed the colors, mirroring the darkness spreading within his soul. A blurred figure came down the street, barely discernible through the thick smog. With a deep sigh, he turned away from the window and returned to a desk cluttered with important documents and notes.

Marcus Leonard had grown up in a household where political discussions at dinner were commonplace. His father had once looked him firmly in the eyes and said, "One day, you will follow in my footsteps and achieve great things." Those words had etched themselves deep into Leonard's consciousness, shaping his future path. His mother was a gentler and more empathetic person, teaching him the importance of compassion and social responsibility. These mixed influences formed him and enabled him to have a deep understanding of social and economic issues.

Leonard had indeed followed in his father's footsteps, studying Law at the university in Plainfield, his hometown from which he could never detach himself. He had started his political career with great enthusiasm, driven by the determination to advance Plainfield's economic boom. In the early years, he had achieved many successes by promoting investments and minimizing bureaucratic obstacles for industrial expansions. The once quiet Plainfield had come to life as companies built factories and offices. Due to his significant contributions, Leonard was eventually appointed city councilor. Fulfilling his father's vision while embracing his mother's teachings had seemed the right path for him.

Now, in the silence of his study, he could no longer deny how one-sided his focus had been. The pride in Plainfield's economic upswing had transformed into crushing guilt as he became aware of the extent of the sacrifices.

The door opened quietly as Claudia entered. "Marcus, you've been working all day. Take a break," she said gently. Her face was pale, and the slight tremor of her hands did not escape him.

"I can't, Claudia. There's so much to do, and I don't know what to do anymore," he confessed.

She stepped closer and placed a hand on his shoulder. "You don't have to carry it all alone," she whispered. "We'll find a way."

He looked into her eyes and recognized both pain and unwavering confidence. "I've made so many mistakes," he said quietly. "And you're paying the price."

Claudia shook her head. She took his hand and squeezed it gently. "We've both made decisions, Marcus. You've always wanted only the best for this city." She smiled weakly. "It's never too late to change something. Trust yourself."

At that moment, they heard the doorbell ring downstairs. "I'll get it." Claudia left the room.

Leonard sat down at his desk, breathing heavily, burying his head in his hands. The burden of his decisions, once seen as triumphs, now pressed on his heart like a heavy stone. The Leonard Effect had once been a symbol of his success, but now he perceived it as synonymous with his failure. The air quality in Plainfield had dramatically worsened, and he knew he bore a large part of the blame. He remembered the year when he had brushed aside the last concerns against building a large factory in Plainfield. Back then, he had been convinced he was doing the right thing. Now, thinking of Claudia's pain-stricken face, he realized that this had been the beginning of the end.

Claudia, his childhood sweetheart and constant companion—his rock in the surf—repeatedly reminded him of what truly mattered: humanity and compassion. But every cough from her cut like a knife through his heart—a constant reminder of his wrong decisions. Her COPD, worsened by air pollution, reflected the direct consequences of his actions. Doubt gnawed at him. *Have I been so wrong? Was my pursuit of success a fatal mistake?* Images of protesting people and polluted streets crowded his mind. *I only wanted the best for Plainfield.*

Downstairs, Leonard heard muffled voices. Claudia was speaking with someone—a visitor he didn't know. At least, he couldn't place the voice. Part of him wanted to go downstairs, to lose himself in her company, away from the oppressive documents on his desk. However, the meeting scheduled for the next day held him back. His sense of duty forced him to stay.

Leonard's gaze fell on the familiar photo of Claudia on his desk. She looked at him with an expression full of understanding and support. *I should have done more, sooner.* Regret gnawed at him as he once again recalled the unintended consequences of his actions—not just for the city but also for his family.

The voices subsided, and the soft closing of the front door caught his attention. The visitor had left, along with the chance for a moment of humanity amid the chaos. He remained seated, alone with his guilt and the oppressive silence.

Reluctantly, he reached for the top report on his desk. The graphs and tables seemed to stare at him, mocking his ignorance. Terms like 'particulate matter pollution' and 'emission units' blurred before his eyes. *I have to understand this. Only then can I change something.*

There was a knock at his office door, and Claudia peeked in. "Marcus, a Mr. Bennet was here. He wanted to speak with you, but he seems to have changed his mind." She hesitated. "He lost his granddaughter. I think he was here looking for answers."

"Oh... I'm sorry," he said quietly. "Did he say how I can reach him?"

Claudia shook her head. "Unfortunately, not. He seemed very upset. Maybe he'll come by again later."

Leonard nodded slowly. "I hope so."

She smiled gently. "I'll let you get back to work now. Remember, you don't have to handle everything alone."

"Thank you, Claudia," he said sincerely.

"If you need a break, I'm about to make some tea."

"That sounds good."

As the silence returned, Leonard felt overwhelmed by the complexity of the task. The scientific data was foreign to him; he had always focused his career on economic matters, delegating environmental issues to others. Now he was sat here, surrounded by technical jargon he barely understood. With a deeply furrowed brow, he grabbed a pen, scribbled frantic notes, crossed them out again, and desperately tried to translate the scientific data into concrete actions.

"No, no, no, this is rubbish!" he cried out in frustration. In a fit of anger, he crumpled up the papers and threw the pen across the room. It hit the wall, leaving a blue line on the plaster—a mute witness to his despair.

Suddenly, it became clear to him: conventional solutions were no longer sufficient. A plan wouldn't suffice, what they needed was a miracle.

At that moment, the phone rang. On the other end was Clara Zheng, head of InnoTech, whose latest development was considered a glimmer of hope. Her voice was calm, though the underlying tension was unmistakable. "Mr. Leonard, we've made a decisive breakthrough and are ready for the next phase."

Leonard sat up, his heart beat faster. The call could change everything. Perhaps this was the chance to make amends for his mistakes. A spark of hope ignited within him, dispelling the darkness for a moment. "Thank you, Ms. Zheng," he said firmly. "Can we meet tomorrow morning? We have no time to lose."

CHAPTER 15
TV-REPORT –
THE NEW TECHNOLOGY

The screen flickered on, displaying the studio of the news channel from Plainfield. Maria Cruz looked into the camera with a warm smile. Her long, distinctive ponytail and dark, expressive eyes gave her an exotic grace, underscored by a confident demeanor.

"Good evening, dear viewers. Today we report on an innovation that can sustainably improve our air quality. Dr. Clara Zheng and her team at InnoTech have developed a technology that is already showing astonishing results." The camera shifted to a pre-produced segment, accompanied by dramatic music. Vivid images of the Gray Winter over Plainfield filled the screen.

Then the scene switched to Clara Zheng in her futuristic laboratory. Surrounded by state-of-the-art technology, she exuded confidence and optimism. "Our project will usher in a new era of air purification."

Drone footage showed an impressive field test in a heavily polluted district. Clara, proud of the progress, commented on the scenes: "In just a few hours, our groundbreaking technology has significantly improved air quality." Viewers first saw the heavily polluted district and the environmental monitor displaying alarming purple. Then, almost magically, the same place appeared cleaner, and the monitor was now a hopeful orange. The steeply falling lines on a graph illustrated that the concentration of pollutants, such as nitrogen oxides, sulfur dioxides, and particulate matter, had been reduced by up to 70%.

"Our technology is based on a multi-layered membrane, which functions like an invisible vacuum cleaner. It absorbs harmful gases and converts them into harmless compounds, making the air immediately cleaner. Children can play outside again, and older people, as long as they take certain precautions, can enjoy more relaxed walks. Our membranes not only clean the air, they renew the hope for a healthier future.

"Our vision doesn't end here," Clara continued, her eyes shining. "We are working to further reduce pollutant concentrations. Our goal is to bring the environmental monitors into the green zone and achieve air quality that is not just acceptable but healthy." With a smile, she added, "We developed this technology because we firmly believe that science and technology can improve our quality of life. This is just the beginning. Our work will continue, and I am confident that we will see even greater progress soon."

The idea that the environmental monitors, which had previously displayed dismal values, could now indicate a turnaround sparked new hope among viewers. With her groundbreaking technology, Clara Zheng had the potential to end the Gray Winter, giving people confidence that science could bring about profound changes.

Back in the studio, Maria Cruz took a deep breath before turning to the camera with a smile. "This is akin to a last-minute rescue," she said, noticeably relieved. "This advancement could represent a turning point in the fight against air pollution."

Then she switched to Dr. Bruno Hansen, the chief chemist at InnoTech. "Dr. Hansen, can you tell us a little more about how this technology works and why it is so promising?"

Dr. Hansen, an older gentleman with tousled hair and glasses that constantly threatened to slip off his nose, replied, "Yes, of course! Our nano-membrane works like a giant air filter. How it attracts harmful gases from the air and transforms them into harmless substances is similar to how trees convert carbon dioxide into oxygen. The special thing is that this process is very efficient and quick, so the air quality improves immediately." Now entirely in his element, he grabbed a pen and began enthusiastically sketching chemical reactions on a whiteboard. "As you can see here, our membranes bind the nitrogen oxides and convert them through catalytic processes into harmless nitrogen and water. Sulfur dioxides are turned into safe sulfur salts, and so on."

Although the chemical details were probably only understandable to experts, Dr. Hansen's expertise and his boundless enthusiasm left a lasting impression on the viewers.

"Let's hear some voices from the affected area," said Maria Cruz, cutting to residents from the district where the field test had taken place.

An elderly lady was the first to step in front of the camera. "I suffered from severe respiratory problems for years and could rarely leave the house. The air here used to be so stuffy that I could hardly breathe. Since these wonderful devices were installed, the air is clean and fresh. Now I can go for walks every day and smell the flowers without coughing. It feels like I've been given a new life." Her eyes shone, and her joy over the regained freedom was clearly for all to see.

Nearby, a young father played with his son in a bustling playground. "My little Benjamin has cystic fibrosis, and every day used to be a challenge because of the poor air. Now he can finally play outside again, but he still wears a mask until the risk score is green—hopefully in the very near future. It's a huge relief," he explained, while the cheerful giggling of his child was heard in the background.

Mikael Vasilakis, introduced as a committed environmental activist, stated, "The new technology has great potential. We are already seeing positive effects, but it currently only combats symptoms. It's important that we accompany it with an addressing the fundamental problems of air pollution. We must not lose sight of the actual causes. The fight for clean air doesn't end here—it is only just beginning. It remains crucial to support research and tackle pollution directly at the source. Only together can we ensure that these successes are not just a fleeting glimmer of hope, but the the beginning of real, sustainable change."

The camera panned to Dr. Marcus Leonard's office, where he was surrounded by environmental studies and legislative proposals. "The successes of this technology show that economic progress and environmental protection can go hand in hand. We must now take responsibility because the future of our cities depends on our decisions. It motivates me to realign our policies and promote the development of innovative, sustainable solutions."

The program returned to Clara Zheng, who stood in her laboratory. "This is just the beginning," she said enthusiastically, her optimism contagious. "We are already planning the next phase, one where we want to deploy our technology in other cities. Our goal is not only to reduce air pollution but also to increase the quality of life for millions of people worldwide."

"Dr. Zheng and her team are working tirelessly to realize their vision of a cleaner, healthier world," Maria Cruz summarized, her eyes shining with excitement. "What impresses me most is her strong commitment and sincere concern for people's well-being. The initial results of this technology are encouraging—a clear sign that we are on the right path.

"Let's hear another perspective. Dr. Hannah Kowalski from the Institute of Environmental Technology and Climate Research, what can you tell us about the recent breakthroughs at InnoTech?"

The camera shifted to Hannah, who stood in her brightly lit laboratory, surrounded by blinking monitors and advanced research equipment. "The improvements in air quality achieved by this new technology show us that significant progress is possible and that science and innovation are extremely helpful tools in fighting our environmental crisis."

She paused briefly, letting her gaze sweep over the equipment before continuing emphatically: "This technological development should not only be seen as a victory for science but as a call to action. It's time for each of us to look beyond our own horizon and play our part. By changing our daily habits and living in a more environmentally friendly way, we can all contribute to better air quality and preserve our environment for future generations." Looking firmly into the camera, she added, "Every act counts and has immense significance."

Hannah concluded her remarks with a motivating appeal: "We have seen what is possible through new technological solutions. Now it's up to us to build on this momentum, turning it into concrete, everyday actions. Every contribution, no matter how small, is crucial. Together, we can shape a world where clean air is not the exception but the norm."

The camera slowly pulled away, and the studio came back into focus. Maria Cruz leaned forward slightly, her eyes fixed on the lens. With a thoughtful nod, she addressed the viewers: "An important appeal from Dr. Hannah Kowalski that we should all take to heart. Every action counts. Stay informed and engaged." Her voice conveyed a mixture of determination and hope that shaped the tone of the broadcast.

With one last optimistic smile, the presenter concluded, "In times like these, every progress is a step out of the darkness. May the initiative of Clara Zheng and her team serve as inspiration for all of us!"

CHAPTER 16
HANNAH KOWALSKI –
WARNINGS ARE IGNORED

Hannah let her gaze wander through the newly opened garden restaurant, while Simon Carson leaned back, relaxed with a mischievous grin. Her eyes swept over the tables and the terrace canopy—everything seemed unremarkable, nothing caught her eye. Finally, her eyes rested on the streetlights lining the avenue.

"The streetlights?" she asked hesitantly, raising her eyebrows.

Simon's grin widened until it lit up his entire face. "Exactly! The membrane is hidden in their upper casing. It sucks in the air, purifies it, and releases it again—completely unnoticed."

Hannah shook her head in disbelief. "I would never have thought that," she murmured, impressed. "You really can't see it."

"That's the genius of it," Simon explained proudly. "The membranes blend inconspicuously into the cityscape. We've hidden them in the flowerboxes along the street and even behind traffic signs and billboards."

A warm smile crossed Hannah's face. Simon's zest for life and enthusiasm were precisely the qualities she had missed in recent weeks. "Tell me, how was it at InnoTech? Are you even coming back to the institute?"

Simon's expression changed slightly, losing its usual sparkle. "It was an incredibly intense time at InnoTech," he began quietly, almost hesitantly. "We practically worked around the clock. And now, well, I'm almost constantly on the road talking about the technology. It's... indescribable. I mean, who gets the chance to be part of something that could save the world?"

Hannah held his gaze firmly, searching for the answer Simon still owed her.

A hint of embarrassment reflected in his eyes. "To be honest," he finally began, "I don't know yet if I'm coming back. Clara Zheng has offered me a permanent position. It's a once-in-a-lifetime opportunity..."

Hannah felt her heart skip a beat. She tried to hide her shock but failed. "You're leaving?"

"Probably," Simon replied, avoiding eye contact. "It would be a significant role in further developing the technology and... well... the work there is incredibly exciting, but I haven't decided yet."

Hannah's thoughts raced. The idea that Simon might leave the institute—and thereby her—for good gave her an unexpected pang. A feeling of loss spread within her, but she didn't want Simon to notice. So, she forced a smile. "That's... great for you, Simon. Really. We'll miss you."

"Thank you," Simon said quietly as he looked back into her eyes, giving her a charming smile. "That means a lot to me. But don't worry, nothing is decided yet. I just didn't want to keep it from you."

Hannah nodded slowly, but inside, everything tightened up. She leaned back and stared up at the bright blue sky, trying to hold on to the moment—perhaps one of the last they could share so carefree.

"Oops, it's late already!" Simon suddenly jumped up. "Hannah, we have to go. My presentation starts in 15 minutes!"

Laughing, they packed their things and hurried to the institute. Simon's words echoed incessantly in Hannah's thoughts, and the laughter they shared had a bitter aftertaste.

Two hours later, he finished his presentation on the new technology. The seminar room at the Institute for Environmental Technology and Climate Research was filled to the last seat, and animated murmurs could be heard. Simon reached into his backpack and pulled out an elegantly designed box. With a fluid motion, he opened it and took out a prototype of the new technology. The attendees marveled as their eyes fell on the small device.

"The technology comes in various sizes," Simon explained, handing the prototype to a spectator. "This is a smaller model. Inside, you can see the membrane." The scientists leaned forward curiously, their eyes following the device as it passed through the rows. Each person turned it in their hands and examined it thoroughly while eagerly taking notes. Simon's voice broke the silence: "Are there any questions?" The sincere interest and enthusiasm of the attendees was unmistakable.

After the lecture, Hannah walked back to the control room, lost in thought. She settled in front of blinking monitors tirelessly displaying data on air quality in different parts of the city. Simon's presentation had raised more questions for her than it had provided answers. With her solid knowledge of chemistry and materials science, she knew all too well that complex technologies like the multilayered nanomembrane did not come without challenges. She was particularly concerned by the fact that catalysts could lose efficiency under extreme conditions.

Her fingers glided almost automatically over the keyboard as she analyzed the current air quality data. So far, she had considered the progress of the technology a success, but now she was specifically looking for irregularities. A few days earlier, a heatwave had occurred in Plainfield, followed by a sudden rain shower. Hannah pulled up the data from that period and discovered slight fluctuations in pollutant levels. They weren't dramatic, but noticeable enough to catch her attention. Could it be that the catalysts were less effective under certain conditions?

A feeling of unease crept over her. As a scientist, it was her responsibility to pursue these leads, even if it meant addressing unpopular truths.

Determined, Hannah picked up the phone and contacted the Ministry of the Environment. After jumping through some bureaucratic hoops, she was finally connected with an appropriate official. In a calm voice, she presented her concerns: "The data is promising, but there are signs of irregularities. Under certain conditions, the catalysts don't seem to function optimally, which could potentially compromise the efficiency of this technology."

She heard a deep sigh on the other end of the line. "Dr. Kowalski, I understand your concerns," the official replied wearily. "However, people are suffering and we're under enormous pressure to deliver quick results. Official reports show a clear improvement in air quality. We should focus on that."

Hannah was not so easily dismissed and pressed on: "This is not just about current measurements but about the long-term stability of the technology. If the catalysts fail under extreme conditions, we could face serious problems. We can't ignore that."

The official responded sharply, "Ms. Kowalski, the data speaks clearly. According to it, air quality is noticeably better. We can't panic over every little irregularity. Perhaps you should step back a bit and acknowledge the successes instead of constantly questioning them. It almost seems like personal resentment is influencing your perspective."

Hannah felt her face grow hot with anger and frustration. The insinuation that her scientific integrity could be clouded by envy or personal feelings struck her deeply. However, she forced herself to remain calm and took a deep breath. "It's not about personal ambition for me. It's about protecting everyone's health and safety. I just want to ensure that we act responsibly and don't overlook any risks."

The official let his impatience openly show. "Ms. Kowalski, your dedication is commendable, but perhaps you should take a break. It seems like you're getting too caught up in this matter. Relax."

This final remark left Hannah speechless. She felt her legitimate concerns were being dismissed for political and bureaucratic reasons. Undeterred, she dialed Clara's number.

Always calm and prudent, Clara listened as Hannah described her worries, only replying after hearing her out. "Hannah, I understand your concern. We've tested this technology for years under various conditions. I can assure you that we take potential risks very seriously. It's true that in some particularly heavily polluted areas, the catalysts reach their limits. In such cases, our observations have shown that absorption into the membrane is slightly delayed, but we were still able to demonstrate a significant reduction in pollutants. Sometimes theoretical models see problems that don't weigh as heavily in practice. You know how rigorously we've tested our technology, even under extreme conditions. Trust us, we have everything under control and are constantly monitoring the situation."

Hannah's hands clenched into fists as, once again, she felt her warnings were being dismissed, but then she paused. Doubts began to gnaw at her. *Have I gone too far? Have I gotten lost in a scientific dead end? Am I letting myself be unsettled by theoretical models that aren't relevant in reality?* But her scientific intuition couldn't be easily suppressed. It was her responsibility to pursue these questions, even if it meant swimming against the tide.

Determined, she grabbed her laptop, typing out a message to Simon. *Hey, can I borrow the membrane prototype you showed earlier? I want to take a closer look at it.* The response came almost instantly. *Sure thing! It's in my former lab. Help yourself.* She exhaled in relief and set off to retrieve it, happy that he was not there to ask any questions. Back in her lab, as she held it in her hands, she was overcome by a feeling of betrayal, as if she were acting behind his back. But the truth was too important to ignore. So, she set about preparing everything for the stress test in her lab. Carefully, she set up the test environment and adjusted the equipment to simulate various extreme scenarios—scenarios in which she feared the catalysts might fail. Inserting the membrane into the test apparatus required utmost precision, but her hands worked calmly and steadily, her fingers obeying without the slightest tremor. Fortunately, her MS symptoms had completely subsided, and she was grateful that her body wasn't letting her down today.

Suddenly, she heard a familiar voice behind her. "What are you doing?" Simon asked quietly, visibly surprised but also with a hint of concern in his voice.

Hannah started when she noticed his sudden presence. Her heart beat faster; she felt as if she'd been caught doing something forbidden. How was she supposed to explain this to him? "Simon... I..." She lowered her gaze, hesitated, and then continued: "I have to run these tests. I have concerns about the membrane's stability under extreme conditions."

Simon's eyes narrowed and a shadow passed over his face. Disappointment and hurt mingled in his expression. "What concerns?" he asked, his voice barely more than a whisper. The tension in his words was unmistakable. "We've tested this technology under every conceivable condition. Do you really think I missed something?"

Hannah felt the weight of his words and hesitantly took a step toward him. "It's not that I'm questioning your work," she said gently, trying to calm him. "But as scientists, we always have to consider all possibilities. What if we've actually overlooked something? I just want to be sure." Her voice trembled, and genuine concern reflected in her eyes.

Simon shook his head. "You know," he began quietly, "I thought there was something between us... something special..." He paused as though searching for the right words. "Trust, Hannah. I thought we trusted each other, but obviously I was mistaken." Staring at her, his voice grew harder. "It hurts to know that you doubt me so much—not just my work but me as a person."

Hannah's heart skipped a beat as she felt the coldness in his words. "Simon, please understand me. My feelings for you don't change the fact that I have to fulfill my responsibility. It's not about you. It's about ensuring that we don't make mistakes— mistakes that could endanger lives."

The silence between them stretched out, heavy and unbearable. Simon's disappointment gave way to a bitter, unyielding expression. "I never thought it would end like this between us." The air between them seemed to tighten with every heartbeat. "I'm going to accept the position at InnoTech. At least there, I know my work is appreciated."

Hannah felt her throat tighten, and tears welled up in her eyes. "Simon, please... I didn't mean for this to happen." Her voice almost broke as she reached out a hand to him, but Simon stepped back.

He turned abruptly and left the lab without another word. His footsteps echoed down the empty corridor until they gradually faded away. Hannah was left alone. The lab, which had previously been her sanctuary, suddenly felt cold and unfamiliar. The monitors blinked indifferently; the hum of the equipment now sounded threatening. She closed her eyes briefly and took a deep breath. She knew she had to conduct the tests. But the price for it seemed higher than she had ever expected.

CHAPTER 17
TV-REPORT –
A NEW ERA OF IMPROVEMENTS

Maria Cruz appeared on the screen with a radiant smile. "Good news from Plainfield! Clara Zheng and her team at InnoTech have developed a revolutionary air purification technology that has already noticeably improved air quality. Our environmental monitors now show values that remain stable in the yellow zone—a milestone in the fight against the Gray Winter."

Scenes from the recent past were presented, showing people hurrying through smog-laden streets wearing breathing masks, the burden of polluted air visible in their tired faces. Like a heavy curtain falling to reveal a new stage, these bleak images were replaced by radiant scenes from the present, with children playing without masks in parks, and cafés where cheerful guests enjoyed the clear weather. The contrast was overwhelming.

"As you can see," Maria continued in a voice marked by euphoria, "the introduction of the air purification technology has not only improved our air but also our lives. It feels as if we are transitioning from the endless Gray Winter into a bright spring."

The focus was now directed to personal stories: a young

couple strolling and laughing through lively streets, a group of students cheerfully playing in the schoolyard, and a family gathering in a newly opened café. "These improvements have enabled us to return to a normal life," explained Maria, as the camera panned over bustling shopping streets and markets. "Shops and schools are open again, and our streets are filled with life."

The report then switched to an outdoor scene, where Maria Cruz stood in a dense forest with Peter Wagner, a long-time forester of the region. The air was clear, and the chirping of birds in the treetops created a peaceful, almost magical atmosphere—a sharp contrast to the former gloom.

"The impacts of the Gray Winter were not only dramatic for us humans," he began as they walked side by side along a narrow path. "Wildlife also suffered greatly. At its worst, I had to pick up dead animals every day—foxes, birds, squirrels..." He paused for a moment, his face reflecting the pain of those past experiences. "My forester's heart bled. Especially the more sensitive species who had no chance against the toxic air."

He pointed to the forest floor. Fresh tracks were imprinted in the soft soil. "See those? They are the footprints of wild boars, an entire family with piglets. At least five, I would estimate." A hint of joy softened his hard features somewhat. "A few months ago, you would hardly have found such tracks. The animals had retreated deep into the underbrush to escape the polluted air, because there the air was cleaner and less contaminated by the city."

Maria knelt down to examine the tracks more closely, her fingers gently brushing over the impressions in the ground. "And now they're coming back?" she asked, visibly moved by the discovery.

Wagner nodded, a smile playing on his lips. "Yes, the animals are slowly returning to their old territories. They're venturing out again, searching for food. Nature is recovering, but it needs our protection."

As they continued walking, Wagner looked up and pointed to a flock of birds circling high above the trees. "The song of the birds was silent for a long time," he explained. "But now you can hear it again—robins, blackbirds, tits. It's as if nature is breathing a sigh of relief. And now it's up to us to ensure it stays that way. We must treat nature with the necessary respect."

Back in the studio, Maria Cruz appeared in front of the camera once more. "The return of the animals and the regeneration of the forest are further signs that our environment is on the path to healing. The positive changes brought about by the new air purification technology affect not only us humans but the entire ecosystem."

A brief cut showed Clara Zheng and her team in front of InnoTech's main building. The efforts of the last weeks were visible: slight shadows under their eyes and tired smiles revealing the long nights and hard work they had invested. At the same time, relief and pride were clearly evident on their faces. "The positive response from our community is not only a confirmation but also an incentive," said Clara, emotionally. "We are proud of what we've achieved, but we must not rest on our laurels. After the successful completion of the field tests, we have expanded the use of our technology to larger areas in and around Plainfield. There is still much work ahead of us, as we need to sustainably secure these improvements and achieve further progress."

The program showed brief interviews with citizens expressing their relief and joy over the changes. "It's great to be back in the classroom again," said Ian Becker, smiling in the schoolyard. "Online teaching was a challenge for all of us, but now everything feels as it should be. I'm happy to have the students in front of me again and to work directly with them. Today, we planted trees in the city park to make a small contribution to the renewal of our city. These trees symbolize the new beginning we are all experiencing here."

Marlene, an elderly lady, was on her way to one of the reopened cafés. "I can't wait to see my friends again," she said, beaming with joy. "For months, we could only talk to each other on the phone, but today we're finally sitting together again. It's an indescribable feeling of delight. My thanks go to the scientists who made this possible and breathed new life into Plainfield."

The camera followed her as she entered the café. Through the windows, you could see her embracing her friends with tears of joy in her eyes. Their faces shone with happiness at the long-awaited reunion.

The camera switched to a rural scene featuring the Hawkins family as the main actors. Once forced to relocate their agricultural activities to an indoor facility, the family members now stood again in their fields. The camera showed them confidently sowing the first seeds. "It feels great to be able to work outside again without fear of the air we breathe," explained Samuel Hawkins, the eldest son, as he inspected a handful of soil. "These advancements give us hope for the upcoming harvest and for the future of our farm."

At the conclusion of the program, Maria Cruz appeared on the screen once more and declared with a grateful smile, "Before we end this broadcast, we also want to thank those who often remain in the background but play an indispensable role in our community. A special thanks goes to the cleaning teams who have tirelessly worked to free our streets from the remnants of the Gray Winter. Their commitment has significantly contributed to not only allowing our city to breathe but also to shine."

The newscast ended with a scene showing a young couple watching the sunrise in the city park. "As we welcome this new morning," Maria said, "we remember the dark days of the Gray Winter. Through joint commitment and constant innovation, a brighter future is finally within reach. Clara Zheng and her team have made it possible for us to look into a future where fresh air and a clear sky are no longer dreams but represent our new reality."

CHAPTER 18
MIKAEL VASILAKIS –
NEW PATHS

Mikael sat alone on a park bench, watching the people strolling through the park on this radiant day. The sky was clear, and the air fresh, both luxuries he had long deemed impossible. He thought of the days of intense activism—the protests under gray skies, and endless campaigns for better environmental policies. The anger that once drove him had given way to a quiet satisfaction, but in this calm, he felt an unexpected emptiness. With the recent success of technology, the urge to protest had waned, causing him to wonder what his role in Plainfield should now be.

An older man sat down next to Mikael on the bench. He appeared friendly, but his stooped back and deep wrinkles revealed a life full of experiences. They both remained silent for a while until the man finally spoke softly.

"Beautiful day today, isn't it?" A slight smile appeared on his lips as he watched the children playing.

Mikael nodded and turned his face to the fresh wind, as if savoring the clear air after the long, bleak times. "Yes, it is. And the people... they seem to have hope again."

The man was quiet for a moment, appearing to weigh his next words carefully. "I was an engineer," he began. "For years, I worked on things that ultimately destroyed more than they benefited. Back then, I thought I was doing the right thing, but now... now I see the price we all had to pay. I was part of the problem. The weight of this guilt is hard to bear."

"I understand," Mikael said. He looked at the man more closely now. His face, his entire demeanor, was marked by deep sorrow. "You're not alone. Many of us have made mistakes, but perhaps... perhaps we now have a second chance."

The man turned to Mikael and looked him directly in the eyes. "This progress we're experiencing now... it's fragile. It's not enough to sit back contentedly and believe everything is okay. It requires mindfulness, constant vigilance. If we're not careful, we'll find ourselves back on the brink faster than we think."

Mikael let the words resonate within him. He felt the weight of their truth. "Perhaps you're right," he said after a while, nodding. "Maybe I should stop fighting and instead start waking people up, so they understand how important it is to stay alert."

"I'm sure you'll find a way," the old man said, standing up and extending his hand. Mikael felt the man hold the handshake a moment longer than would be typical. "My name is Robert Bennet."

Mikael opened his mouth to introduce himself, but the man was quicker: "Mikael Vasilakis. I know who you are."

With these words, Bennet turned and walked away slowly, as if carrying a heavy burden. Mikael remained seated, his gaze fixed on the departing man. Something inside him had been set in motion, deeply moved by the encounter that had come so unexpectedly.

He was lost in thought when he suddenly heard his name. "Mikael!" Hannah's voice snapped him out of his reverie. He looked up and spotted her in the crowd. Purposefully, she approached him, smiling and waving.

"Hello, Hannah, have a seat," Mikael said, patting the bench invitingly beside him. "How are you?"

"Quite well," she replied as she sat down. "It's nice to breathe fresh air again without constantly thinking about work."

"Speaking of work," Mikael began thoughtfully, "what do you think of the technology? I mean, it's achieved a lot, but..." He shrugged and looked at her questioningly.

Hannah sighed softly and furrowed her brow. "It's impressive what Clara Zheng and her team have accomplished, no question, but I remain skeptical. We found a solution so quickly that the long-term consequences are hardly researched. I mean, who knows what could happen in a few years?"

Mikael nodded, his thoughts aligning with hers. "You're right. I can't really keep up technically—I never finished my studies. But if the whole thing falters at some point, there's still your project with the biofilms, right? How's that going?"

Hannah slowly shook her head. "My biofilm project was discontinued after an accident in the lab destroyed everything. Years of work were suddenly lost. And now that the air is clean, our sponsors no longer believe in the necessity of further research. It feels as if all my efforts were in vain."

She gazed into the distance, and Mikael could see the disappointment in her eyes. Hannah brushed a strand of hair from her face. "And what are you doing now? It seems like neither of our work is needed anymore."

Mikael gave a faint smile. "I'm just thinking about what I should do next. Maybe it's time to focus more on education. People need to understand that they have to remain vigilant, even if the air is clean."

Hannah's eyes widened with enthusiasm. "That's a fantastic idea, Mikael! Let me know if you need any help."

She stood up, a joyful glow on her face. "I have to go now—I'm visiting my parents. My father is finally doing better, and the two of them are really blossoming. It feels so good to see them like this."

She paused briefly, as if another thought had come to her. "Oh, and how is your neighbor? Has he recovered?" she asked.

Mikael slowly shook his head. "Unfortunately, not." For a moment, both were silent, each lost in thought. Finally, Mikael continued, "I have to go too. I'll get in touch if I need support.

First, I need to come up with a rough concept."

"Do that," Hannah replied gently. She gave him one last, encouraging smile before she said goodbye. Mikael remained seated for a moment longer; his thoughts were already beginning to revolve around initial ideas that were slowly taking shape.

A little later, he entered one of the new cafés now springing up all over the city like mushrooms. He scanned the room until he spotted her in a corner: Maria Cruz. The light of the afternoon sun gently played around her dark hair. It enveloped her in a golden glow from which he couldn't avert his eyes. A warm feeling spread within him.

Mikael couldn't suppress the smile that crept onto his lips. "There's the woman I've been waiting for all day. Nice to see you again, Maria."

She stood up, smiled, and gave him a light kiss on the cheek.

After he sat down, Mikael let his gaze wander over the sunny streets outside. "Looks like we've finally left the Gray Winter behind us." With a wink, he added, "Now it's time to enjoy spring before it changes its mind." They both laughed easily and soon dove into a lively conversation. Together, they dreamed of a better future as the worries and stress of the past months slowly faded. The hours flew by, filled with stories and laughter over memories of their first encounters.

"Tell me, did everything go well back then at the demo?" Maria asked, looking at him curiously.

Mikael grinned wryly and leaned back. "You mean the demo where we first met? I wouldn't say it exactly went well..."

"Oh no," laughed Maria. "What happened?"

"Well, a little scuffle broke out, and before I knew it, I was lying unconscious on the ground—in handcuffs. When I came to, I was in a police car."

Maria stared at him, utterly baffled. "You were knocked unconscious and were in handcuffs?"

Mikael shrugged as if it were nothing special. "Well, that's how it goes when you're on the police's list. They'd been after me for a while and were just looking for an excuse to take me to the station. Leonard probably helped them along quite a bit."

"And what happened then?" Maria asked, her voice now filled with more concern than curiosity.

"Nothing wild. An interrogation, a few questions, and then they let me go after a few hours—not without giving me a little lecture about how dangerous my activities were." He shrugged again. "The usual."

Maria shook her head and laughed. "And you put it so casually…"

Mikael grinned broadly. "What can I say? It wasn't my first visit to the station—and probably won't be the last."

Maria burst into hearty laughter. "You never told me that."

Their conversation grew deeper as they discussed the significance of their work and the changes they wanted to bring about in the world. Maria paused for a moment, looking at Mikael seriously. "What will you do now that there's nothing left to protest about?" she asked softly.

Mikael smiled and sipped his coffee. "I've been thinking about it. It's time to make people realize how important it is to stay vigilant. The technology has improved a lot, but we must not become complacent. Otherwise, we'll quickly be back where we started." Maria looked at him with interest, and Mikael continued, "I'm considering starting an environmental education initiative: workshops, lectures, maybe even a podcast. People need to understand that each individual can make a difference."

Maria leaned forward. "That's a great idea, Mikael. I have something similar in mind—a documentary about how quickly we forget and the dangers that brings." She played with a strand of hair slipping through her fingers. "Maybe we could collaborate?"

Mikael met her gaze. "Collaborate? That sounds... very promising."

"Exactly, that's what I thought too," Maria replied with a mischievous tone. "You bring the passion, and I have the platform to spread the message. We'd be an unbeatable team, wouldn't we?"

A single glance between them was enough to cement their growing closeness. Mikael calmly placed his hand on the table and gently took Maria's hand in his. Their eyes met, and for a moment, everything else seemed to stand still. Both smiled slightly, a bit embarrassed, but a quiet familiarity hung in the air. The touch was tentative, yet it spoke more than a thousand words.

Time flew by as the sun slowly disappeared behind the horizon and the first stars appeared in the evening sky. They continued exchanging ideas and thoughts, their connection growing ever stronger. Finally, Mikael stood up and led Maria outside.

Hand in hand, they walked along the street, the soft light of the streetlights casting warm, golden shadows on the path. "You know, Mikael," Maria said as she moved closer to him, "I have a feeling that this is the beginning of something special."

"So do I," he replied, unable to suppress a smile. The warm feeling in his chest was more than satisfaction—it was the sense of finally having arrived. The city, slowly recovering from the hardships of the Gray Winter, offered them the perfect backdrop for a new beginning. In that moment, Mikael knew he was no longer alone.

CHAPTER 19
CLARA ZHENG –
CELEBRATING SUCCESS

Clara Zheng stood in the midst of the festively decorated hall, observing as guests gradually arrived. A journalist pushed through the crowd toward her, holding out a microphone. "Ms. Zheng, how does it feel to have given humanity a future?"

Clara paused. Her thoughts drifted to the countless hours she and her team had spent in the lab—the sleepless nights, the endless experiments, the almost overwhelming setbacks, and the many canceled personal engagements that had driven her further into isolation. She took a deep breath and smiled. "It's hard to put it into words," she began, her voice calm and controlled. "This journey was anything but easy. There were times when we wondered if our work would ever lead to success, but now, standing here and seeing people breathe freely again, I feel a deep gratitude—not just for the success but also for the dedication of my team and the hope we're bringing into the world."

The journalist nodded, clearly impressed. "What were the biggest challenges you had to face?"

Clara considered. "The biggest challenges? Well, we faced technical problems that demanded a lot of ingenuity, and financial constraints that nearly forced us to give up more than once. What kept us going was the awareness that we have a responsibility—not just to our generation but those that follow."

"How safe is your technology in the long term? Are there no risks?"

Clara smiled professionally as the warning call from Hannah Kowalski flashed through her mind. To dispel any remaining doubts, she had ordered additional tests. After a record-breaking two weeks, the results were in—the membrane was safe in the long term. She looked calmly at the journalist and answered firmly, "We've conducted extensive tests, both internally and externally, under a wide range of conditions. You can be sure that we've left nothing to chance."

"Thank you, Ms. Zheng," said the journalist with a respectful nod. "Your work has changed the world."

Clara returned his nod with a smile and then turned away. The hall was gradually filling up, and the noise level was rising. She sensed the expectant excitement and curiosity of the guests eagerly awaiting her presentation.

As the last people took their seats, the lights in the hall dimmed. The murmuring subsided as Clara stepped onto the stage, and the audience's attention focused intently on her. She cast a final glance at the before-and-after pictures on the walls— powerful testimonies of what her team had achieved.

Clara raised the microphone and began, her voice calm and determined, exuding the unwavering control she always strived for: "Good evening, ladies and gentlemen. Today, we are not just celebrating a technological achievement but the beginning of a new era of hope for our planet." She let her gaze sweep over the audience, pausing briefly at the children in the front row. "These children here, breathing freely and carefree, are the reason we undertook all of this. They are the future, making every sleepless night, every experiment, and every challenge worthwhile, because they deserve a world where clean air is not a privilege but a given."

The audience broke into applause, but Clara remained composed. "Developing this technology was anything but a straightforward path. There were setbacks and doubts. Many told us it was impossible, but that didn't discourage us. On the contrary, it gave us the will and strength to work even harder. We knew there was no alternative. Our planet, our children—they deserve the best. Today, we see the result of these collective efforts."

The audience hung on her every word, with the impact reflected in their captivated faces. But just before Clara intended to conclude her speech, she noticed a man at the edge of the hall. His long gray coat set him apart from the other guests, giving him an unsettling aura. His eyes fixed on her with an intensity that threw her off balance. Clara felt a shiver run down her spine. She didn't need to guess who he was or why he was here—she knew instantly.

Clara blinked, and her heart pounded so fiercely she thought everyone in the room could hear it. She tried to focus on her words. "These challenges have bonded us as a team... and shown that no obstacle is too great when we believe in a common goal." Her voice sounded firmer than she felt, and although she appeared outwardly composed, her hands were shaking and her knees weakening.

As the applause swelled, Clara attempted to put on her usual smile, but it wouldn't quite come. Instead, her gaze pierced the crowd, searching for the man in the gray coat. He was gone. She forced herself to maintain her composure, ignoring the trembling in her limbs as she stood upright and proud on the stage—a strong woman who couldn't afford any weakness, regardless of the inner helplessness she felt.

During the subsequent reception, Clara mingled with the crowd, accepting people's congratulations and engaging in animated conversations with politicians and sponsors. The atmosphere was filled with enthusiasm and joy, while Clara endeavored to conceal her inner turmoil. The evening appeared to have gone perfectly so far.

A waiter approached her, and she took a glass of champagne from his tray. "This is also for you," he said, handing her a folded note. Clara accepted it wordlessly and discreetly glanced around.

Near the exit, she spotted the man in the gray coat. He held her gaze briefly, then turned and walked out the door. A cold shiver shot through her. She had feared this moment would come—that her past would catch up with her, just when the whole world was watching. Striving not to reveal anything, she continued to smile, but her thoughts were now elsewhere.

As the event concluded and the last guests left the hall, Clara stood alone by the window, gazing out over the city whose air was now clear again. She unfolded the note, her hands shaking slightly. Its contents confirmed her worst fears: what she had kept hidden for so long now threatened to come to light.

It had been just a test in a remote mountain region. She couldn't have known that a school class was there, but the images... those gruesome images in the media. The staring eyes and lifeless bodies still haunted her nightmares—relentless and tormenting—a constant companion to her guilt. No one knew what had really happened except for Clara, her closest associates, and the man.

I know everything, and soon the world will know too.

No threat, no ultimatum—just those words. The note was clear: the moment of truth was approaching. How much time did she have before it all went public? Cold sweat broke out on her forehead as her stomach knotted. *The world will see me as a monster, not their savior.*

"Here you are, hiding!" Simon Carson approached her. His green eyes shone with joy and the champagne he'd consumed during the reception. "It feels so good to finally see all the hard work paying off."

As Simon beamed cheerfully at her, she felt a lump in her throat. She wanted to tell him everything, but the words wouldn't come. Instead, she forced herself to smile. "Yes, it does. Thank you for your support, Simon. Without you and the team, this wouldn't have been possible."

Simon nodded enthusiastically. "Thank you, Clara. Come on, the others are waiting downstairs. Let's celebrate our success!"

A strained smile flickered across her face. She allowed herself to be swept up in Simon's excitement, but the oppressive weight in her chest did not ease. Clara tried to push aside her mounting anxiety and enjoy these last few hours, unsure of what the next day would bring.

CHAPTER 20
MARCUS LEONARD –
NEW PATHS IN ENVIRONMENTAL POLICY

In the state-of-the-art conference hall of the government building, the leading minds of the province gathered for a decisive meeting on environmental policy. Dr. Marcus Leonard, city councilor and economic expert, glanced briefly at his notes. He didn't need further preparation; speaking was his strength, and he knew exactly what he wanted to say.

He recalled a recent conversation with his old school friend, Henry, which had inspired these considerations. With a worried expression, Henry, who now ran an industrial enterprise, had warned him: "Marcus, industry is at a standstill, many jobs are at risk. We urgently need more leeway with environmental regulations so we can be productive again."

Leonard had nodded thoughtfully. "I understand, Henry, but we also have to consider people's concerns. They are afraid that the situation will deteriorate again. It will be a difficult balancing act."

Henry had patted him encouragingly on the shoulder. "We're counting on you."

In the conference hall, an atmosphere of expectation and

tension prevailed as the participants awaited Leonard's proposals. Leonard stepped calmly and confidently to the podium, his impeccably fitting suit completing the image of a man who knew exactly what effect he wanted to achieve—and did. His thoughts wandered only briefly. *Fortunately, Clara Zheng's technology works so reliably. The air is clean, the issue settled.* The corners of his mouth twitched slightly. *Now it's about the essentials. The economy must be put back on track. Jobs, production, growth—that's what counts.* He brushed aside the brief concerns about the environment. *It's time to steer progress in the right direction.* He took a deep breath and began his speech with his usual determination.

"Esteemed colleagues, thanks to Clara Zheng's groundbreaking technology, our air quality has significantly improved. This opens up the possibility of reconsidering some of the stricter environmental regulations. I would now like to share my ideas with you." With these words, he started his presentation. The projector cast diagrams and statistics onto the wall, illustrating the advantages of each measure.

"Point 1: Increased Operating Times for Public Transportation. Increasing the frequency of public transportation schedules would reduce dependence on private vehicles while simultaneously increasing our citizens' flexibility in daily life.

"Point 2: Introduce Flexibility in Production Requirements. By allowing factories to choose between disposable and reusable items, we can achieve cost savings, faster production times, and relief during the transition phase to sustainable solutions. Since disposable products are cheaper and more convenient for consumers, this could stimulate consumption and strengthen the economy.

"Point 3: Raising Emission Limits for Local Industries. By moderately increasing emission limits, local industry can resume production, contributing to the economic revival of our city. This measure will not only secure jobs but also create new ones. Additionally, we can ensure that air quality standards are still met.

"And now we come to the fourth and most important point: Relaxation of Driving Bans. By gradually relaxing driving bans, we would enable our citizens to have more freedom for family and leisure activities, and the more flexible use of cars for commuting. This will significantly increase quality of life without substantially increasing environmental pollution."

While Leonard spoke, he noticed some of his listeners nodding in agreement, while others frowned skeptically. Harriet Martin, a respected environmental scientist and parliamentarian known for her strict environmental policies, finally raised her hand. "How can we ensure that these relaxations do not endanger our progress in air purification? What if we regress?" Her voice was firm and challenging.

Leonard, who respected Martin's commitment to environmental issues, but was often annoyed by her uncompromising stance, nevertheless took the question seriously. "That is a legitimate concern, Ms. Martin," he replied. He paused briefly to organize his thoughts. "We will introduce these changes as pilot projects and continuously evaluate their impacts."

Harriet Martin nodded, although her expression remained skeptical. "And what exactly will these evaluations look like? Who will conduct them?" she asked further

Leonard felt the eyes of the attendees on him and knew that his answer was crucial. "The monitoring will be carried out by both independent environmental scientists and government agencies. We will regularly publish reports to ensure transparency and make sure everyone is fully informed."

Harriet Martin seemed to appreciate the efforts for transparency. "I will closely monitor the implementation of these projects, Mr. Leonard. We must ensure that we do not act shortsightedly just because the current data is promising. We don't want a second Leonard Effect."

Leonard skillfully ignored the jab, even though it struck him. "Your critical eye sharpens us all, Ms. Martin. I look forward to ongoing discussions with you and other colleagues, in the common endeavor to ensure that our policies remain both environmentally conscious and realistic."

He paused briefly before continuing: "Next, I will add some points about industry, which has practically come to a standstill in recent years. It is important that we revive it, while of course, taking environmental protection into account." With these words, he nodded to Harriet Martin.

The session ended with lively discussions, indicating that most attendees were convinced by the proposed changes. It was clear that these measures were worth trying, so that a balance could be found between environmental protection, quality of life, and economic development.

CHAPTER 21
YOUNG ADULTS –
THE CALL OF FREEDOM

After weeks of hard effort and relentless pedaling, Lara, Naomi, Alex, Tom, and Basil enjoyed the fresh, clean air that had become part of their journey. Finally, they could ride without masks, and the world shone again in vibrant colors. Although their legs were heavy from months of cycling, they were filled with a joy that almost made them forget how tired they were, and the noticeable change around them gave them new energy.

Since the government had recently relaxed the measures, the streets were filling up again. Cars occasionally crossed their path—a sign that people were using their regained freedoms to leave their homes and participate in social life again.

One afternoon, after several hours of uninterrupted cycling, the teenagers decided to take a well-deserved break at a rest area. They had just stretched out on the benches when a red vintage convertible rolled into the parking lot and stopped near them.

The driver, a cheerful older gentleman with laugh lines around his eyes, got out and stretched contentedly before turning to the teenagers. "Hello, young folks! Where are you headed?"

They looked up, surprised and a bit unsure of how to

respond. Alex cleared his throat and finally answered hesitantly, "We're just following the road."

"Ah, that brings back memories of my old adventures," the man exclaimed with a broad grin as he sat down uninvited on the bench next to them. "I'm Anthony. In my younger years, I explored the world in a similar way." He patted his knees contentedly. "If you're interested, I can tell you some of my stories." The teenagers exchanged quick glances and shrugged. Why not? They had nothing against a little diversion.

Anthony beamed and continued, "Freedom was my compass, and I never worried about anything—certainly not about environmental protection or anything like that."

As the young people shared their snacks with him, Anthony began to tell stories of his travels—wild rides through unknown countries and the many freedoms he had enjoyed. Each story opened a window into a time when today's worries seemed far away. Now, Anthony had captured the teenagers' interest, and they listened intently, curious about what he would say next.

"... and there I was, in the middle of my world trip in South America, with nothing but my old motorcycle and a thirst for adventure. I had just come from a rally through the Atacama Desert. I had been riding for days, and the endless expanse of the desert lay behind me when I got caught in an unexpected storm. The roads turned into muddy tracks, barely passable, but I pushed through. My motorcycle coughed and sputtered as if it had a cold, spitting black smoke like a grumpy dragon. Exhausted and completely soaked, I finally reached a small mountain village. No sooner had I turned off the engine than the village elder approached me." Anthony leaned toward Basil and slightly raised his shoulders, as if he wanted to hide. "Honestly, I felt decidedly uneasy. The elder looked first at my motorcycle, then at me, and suddenly his serious gaze turned into a broad smile. 'Fiesta!' was all he said." Anthony then added with a mischievous smile, "That's all that was needed, and I wouldn't have understood more in Spanish, anyway."

He smiled slyly as he saw the teenagers' enthusiastic expressions. "I will never forget that night. We celebrated until dawn. I danced, ate, and drank with the villagers as if I were one of them. It was one of those magical nights you only experience when you fully surrender to the moment—without a plan, without worries."

He leaned back and continued, "Today, such trips are not contemplated, due to environmental concerns, I know, but back then it was a different time. These experiences showed me how valuable spontaneous human connections are, beyond technology and modern comforts. It's about experiencing life, not just surviving it."

Anthony stood up, brushed the dust off his jeans, and gave the teenagers a radiant smile. "It was nice to reminisce a bit about the old days, but I have to go. My daughter is expecting me, and I have a long drive ahead." He extended his hand, and each of the teenagers shook it warmly.

"Remember," he said, looking into each of their eyes, "life is a collection of moments and stories. Make the most of it and consider going wherever the road takes you. Sometimes it's the unforeseen detour that writes the best stories. Take the paths others don't, because that's where you'll discover what else life has in store for you." With a final wave, Anthony climbed into his red convertible, started the engine, and drove off, his silhouette quickly shrinking as he left only a cloud of smoke behind.

"Seems like he still hasn't gotten rid of the grumpy dragon," joked Basil, who was feeling better by now. The other teenagers laughed and watched the red convertible until it was just a dot on the horizon.

"He really lived..." murmured Naomi, more to herself than to the others.

Tom nodded, visibly moved by the encounter. "Yes, and he reminded me that there's still a lot to experience, even if we try to act environmentally conscious."

They remained sitting on the benches for a while longer, inspired by Anthony's stories and the freedom they expressed. The encounter left a lasting impression that unexpectedly and profoundly changed their view of the journey and what really mattered.

"You know, sometimes I think about the stories my parents told," Naomi began, turning a pebble in her hand. "They talked about how they could just go out and discover the world without fear or restrictions. They often took flights to distant countries, and sometimes they were only away for the weekend. We've never experienced that freedom. It feels somehow unfair that we never got to know that lightheartedness, even if things are better now. We're much too aware of the fragility of our environment."

Basil grinned, always ready with a joke. "Well, I'm fully enjoying it as it is now. Except that my legs are protesting from all this pedaling. They're screaming for a break!"

Lara looked up excitedly. "Maybe we should do a bit of hitchhiking. We really deserve a break from cycling."

Tom frowned. "And what about the fragility of the environment?"

Alex shrugged. "It'll be fine. We can make an exception. After all, we've been traveling by bike for months. We deserve to treat ourselves. Besides, these air filter technologies are really robust. They've been thoroughly tested."

Naomi sighed and let the pebble fall from her hand. "Okay, I'm in."

With a new plan in mind, they made their way to the road, leaving their bicycles at the rest area for the time being. They stuck out their thumbs and waited patiently. The first cars drove by without stopping, but eventually, an older couple in a van pulled over. "Where are you headed?" the driver asked with a warm smile.

"We're following the wind!" Alex enthusiastically shouted, quoting Anthony's words before they got in.

As they drove south, they chatted animatedly about the places they wanted to see, inspired by the adventure stories the old traveler had shared with them. This new freedom seemed to open up a world full of possibilities, just as he had once experienced.

Amid the laughter and new plans, a subtle, unspoken topic arose: With every mile they covered in the van, they moved a little further away from the strict environmental principles that had once inspired their endeavor. The ease of hitchhiking and the joy of experiencing the world in a new, more convenient way slowly pushed aside the memories of their initial environmentally conscious motivations.

As the afternoon drew to a close, a wave of guilt washed over Naomi as she looked out the window at the passing trees. "Are we still on the right path?" she whispered, barely audible over the rushing wind. Similar doubts were reflected in the faces of the others.

In the evening, when they set up camp by a small lake, the teenagers spontaneously decided to take a dip in the cool water, laughing and joking as they dove in. "It feels like we can finally live again, not just survive," called out Alex as they frolicked in the water, enjoying the freedom.

"Look, are those airplane lights?" Lara exclaimed, pointing to the sky.

"That's right," Tom said thoughtfully. "Either we couldn't see them all those years during the Gray Winter, or there really were no airplanes in the sky."

Naomi lay on her back and let herself float in the water; her gaze directed at the starry sky. "And the stars," she whispered. "How long has it been since we've seen them so clearly?"

Tom swam over to her and nodded. "It feels like the world is slowly finding its way back to itself."

Filled with the lightness of the moment, they all agreed. Basil began telling jokes, and soon their laughter echoed across the lake as they enjoyed the cool night air and the feeling of togetherness.

Despite the positive changes and newfound freedoms, a quiet voice in the back of each of their minds reminded them that their actions had consequences. In this moment of rediscovering the world, these concerns seemed distant and were easy to ignore. After a cozy dinner by the campfire, they decided to throw all the remaining leftovers, including the plastic wrappers, into the fire so as not to leave any waste behind. Finally, they fell asleep, accompanied by the gentle lapping of the lake. They dreamed of further adventures as the thought of environmental protection slowly faded into the background.

The gentle rustling of the water mingled with the whispering leaves—a silent reminder that nature was always listening.

CHAPTER 22
ROBERT BENNET – AFTERMATH

Bennet stood at the window of his living room and let his gaze wander over the revitalized city. Children ran along the sidewalks. Their cheerful shouts and the ringing of bicycle bells filled the air—sounds that once seemed so distant. The air was clear, and the colors of the city appeared so vibrant that they almost hurt his eyes. Yet, although the city was blossoming, Bennet felt the deep, unbearable pain pervading inside him.

Each laugh, each playing child brought back memories of Ella. In a world now full of hope, she should have had her place. *Why can't she be here too? Why did she have to leave before the world changed for the better?* These thoughts weighed on him like a heavy burden, and the deep wound in his heart ached relentlessly.

Since Ella's death, he had been trapped in his grief. The regular therapy sessions offered little relief. The tormenting question *Could I have done more?* lingered like a dark shadow. No answer could ease the pain that caused the emptiness in his heart. Tears welled up in his eyes. He let them flow while continuing to watch the lively city.

The progress was undeniable—new air purification systems, a

clear sky, people smiling again. For Bennet, however, these changes had come too late. A bitter smile flickered across his face as the sad realization hit him.

Driven by the need to escape this oppressive mood, he decided to take a walk in the city's newly planted parks. Martha, who now dared to leave the house again, accompanied him. They hoped that a walk in the fresh air might help them find some inner peace. The paths were lined with fresh greenery; flowers bloomed in all colors, and the trees bore young leaves that rustled gently in the wind. Everywhere they saw families and friends sitting on picnic blankets, and children ran on the lawns—the parks a living symbol of a new beginning.

As they walked slowly under the trees, Bennet looked up. "Do you see how the light breaks through the branches? It's strange how it can be so bright and so dark at the same time."

Martha followed his gaze and lifted her face slightly to the cool air. "It's like a constant change, isn't it?" she replied. "One moment sun, the next shadow."

Bennet sighed, his face half in light, half in shadow. "That's exactly how I feel. These bright moments, when I see the children playing and laughing, they fill me with joy. But then comes the shadow—the darkness that reminds me of Ella... It shows me that she will never play in this light again."

Martha smiled at him gently and took his hand. "It's okay to stand in this shadow, Robert. You don't always have to be in the light. The shadow is also a part of life. It makes the bright moments all the more valuable."

Bennet nodded. A fleeting smile crossed his face, illuminated by a sunbeam breaking through. "I know you're right. It's just so hard. You're so wise, Martha, and I'm so glad to have you by my side."

Martha squeezed his hand tighter. "Let's walk together through the light and shadow. We both need to see the whole, so we can heal. Ella wouldn't have wanted us to stand still."

Bennet looked at her as the warm sun cast long shadows behind them on the path. "I'll try, for you and for her."

At the end of a flower-filled path, they took a break. They

stood before a large, colorful poster announcing a city festival. "*Let's celebrate the fresh air! A festival for our future—the Green Spring is here,*" Martha read aloud. The bright colors of the poster radiated an infectious cheerful energy, yet Bennet's expression remained thoughtful, almost melancholic.

Martha noticed his look. "That could be nice, couldn't it?" she said softly, a hint of hope in her voice.

"I know that everyone sees a reason to celebrate..." Bennet began slowly, "but I... I just can't find peace with it." His voice was quiet, marked by unresolved pain.

He noticed a shadow rising in Martha's eyes as well. She must feel the loss just as deeply as he did. And yet, it seemed as if she had decided to look forward, perhaps in the hope that he would one day follow her.

Martha stepped closer to him. Her proximity offered silent support. "I feel the loss every day too, Robert, but I believe Ella would have wanted us to try not to miss the beautiful moments. Maybe the festival will help us see a little light, even if it's just for a moment."

Bennet looked at her, gratitude and sorrow in his eyes. "I wish I could see it that way too, Martha. I wish I could simply be happy and not constantly think of Ella."

"You don't have to stop grieving to participate," Martha replied gently. "It's not about forgetting or pretending nothing happened. Rather, it's about finding a way to move forward despite the pain. Maybe the festival is a small step in that direction."

After a long moment of reflection, Bennet slowly nodded. "Maybe you're right. Maybe that's what we both need—a chance to embrace life again, no matter how hard it may be for us."

With mixed feelings but strengthened by Martha's gentle encouragement, Bennet decided to give the festival a chance— not as an escape from his grief but as a courageous step forward.

That night, as the moon stood high in the sky and the city below him grew quiet, Bennet found no peace in sleep. Instead, he drifted into a deep dream in which he saw Ella in a meadow full of wildflowers. She laughed and waved to him. Her eyes shone with joy, as lively as he remembered them. Bennet ran towards her, but she always seemed a bit farther away. When he finally stopped, panting, he saw Ella in the distance, her lips moving. The wind carried her fateful words to him: "We will see each other again."

CHAPTER 23
PLAINFIELD –
RETURN OF OLD HABITS

After years of restrictions and adjusted consumption, the Walker family decided to celebrate the end of the Gray Winter with an extended picnic in the local park. It was an especially exciting day for the children, Max and Sophie, who could now enjoy the lush greenery of nature together with their parents. For the first time, the whole family was taking a trip outdoors. Max and Sophie ran across the expansive meadows, their laughter and squeals echoing over the grass and audible from afar.

Under a large oak tree, the parents spread out their blanket and unpacked the treats they had brought. Mr. Walker grabbed the plastic cutlery and Styrofoam containers, distributing them to the children, who took a short break. "Finally, a real picnic again! This way, we don't have to carry everything back home and wash it," he said.

As he distributed the food, he thought for a moment. *Environmental protection has severely strained our household budget in recent years. Everything became more expensive, from groceries to everyday items.* He looked at the disposable cutlery he was holding. *Luckily, better availability now makes things much cheaper and more convenient. That leaves more money for other things. Maybe finally a motorcycle. That would be great.* He smiled at the thought of riding along a country road with the wind rushing past him.

After the meal, the children continued to play carefree, chasing each other and laughing across the meadow, while Mr. Walker leaned back and enjoyed the sight of his happy family.

A gust of wind caught some packaging from the trashcan and sent it swirling over the meadow like an uninvited guest. Mrs. Walker watched this with slight unease. "Shouldn't we be more careful?" she asked her husband hesitantly.

Mr. Walker waved it off. "Oh, don't worry. Let's just enjoy today." With that, he sank deeper into the blanket. He felt the sun on his face. The times when they had carefully avoided every piece of waste now seemed distant and irrelevant. "Sometimes you just have to let your soul dangle," he murmured, convinced that small slip-ups in everyday life were insignificant as long as they happened only occasionally.

This indifference reflected the general mood of many city residents. In this moment of carefree enjoyment, the necessity of prudent environmental policy seemed far away. Mr. Walker and his family were not the only ones who gave up some of their environmentally friendly principles for a bit of normality and joy.

After the Walkers finished their picnic, they got back into their car, which they had taken out of the garage for this special day. As they drove through the busy streets back home, Mr. Walker noticed that it wasn't just his family enjoying the newfound freedom. Traffic jammed at every intersection, and the deafening hum of engines filled the streets. Clouds of exhaust fumes drifted, mingling with the scent of freshly cut grass and blooming flowers. The familiar hustle and bustle of traffic, the constant honking, and the soft rattling of old engines had reclaimed their place in the city. The fleeting dream of quiet, low-emission streets had quickly faded, displaced by the return to everyday life. He also saw that cranes were now towering all over the city, and the noise of demolition work and construction machinery filled the streets, as if the city was being rebuilt in the zeal of its newfound freedom. Mr. Walker took a deep breath, grateful for the new technology that made it possible to live a normal life again without having to think constantly about the burden of environmental protection.

Industry was also adapting quickly. Plumes of smoke rose anew from the chimneys of factories that had once switched to more environmentally friendly methods. The demand for cheap, fast solutions was rising again, and some companies resorted to more cost-effective procedures to meet the growing need. Assembly lines rattled, and mass production was running at full speed once more, with all the consequences.

In stores that had completely switched to sustainable products during the worst times, old habits quickly returned. Plastic packaging and disposable products filled the shelves again, gleaming under the neon lights, tempting customers with convenience and, in particular, their price. The more people bought, the cheaper each item became, encouraging customers to load up their shopping carts.

Even the shopping malls, which had once closed their doors, experienced a new boom. Crowds of people streamed through the wide corridors, drawn by flashing signs promising discounts and special offers. The revived consumer enthusiasm drowned out the quiet admonitions of recent months, and ecological mindfulness gave way to a carefree lifestyle.

The parks, considered green oases amid urban renewal, were not safe from old patterns either. After celebrations and gatherings, piles of trash were left behind, nullifying the city administration's efforts to keep the green spaces clean and inviting. The image of neglect stood in sharp contrast to joyful family outings like that of the Walkers, showing how quickly old habits could regain a foothold in a recovering world.

In an especially symbolic part of the city, where a factory had once stood, converted into a museum for sustainable technologies and an education center during the Gray Winter, shadows of the past now appeared. The building, once lovingly restored, had reopened as a factory—no longer a place of knowledge. With the revival of industrial production, the air was once again filled with the dull drone of heavy machinery and thick plumes of emissions. The factory chimneys spewed black smoke into the sky, obscuring the clear contours of the city. An intangible melancholy hung over the area—a silent testament that the fight for a sustainable future was far from won.

As the city fell back into old habits, there were some who noticed the change but did not want to accept it.

As Bennet sat on a sunny afternoon on a park bench, he let his gaze wander over the surroundings. His path had led him past that very factory. He saw a group of teenagers carelessly throwing their trash onto the ground next to an empty garbage can, before disappearing into the overgrown garden of the former Museum for Sustainable Technology, now the scene of a boisterous drinking party. The sight filled him with deep disappointment. "How quickly we forget," he murmured. A wave of sadness washed over him. For a moment, he considered addressing the teenagers, but fatigue and resignation held him back. *What good would it do?* Human nature seemed incorrigibly careless and forgetful, especially regarding the lessons of the recent past.

Then he noticed a little girl in a bright red coat cautiously approaching. She bent down, picked up the crumpled packaging, and threw it into the trashcan. As Bennet watched the little one, a gentle glimmer of hope passed through him. *Maybe not all is lost, after all.* When she noticed him, she became embarrassed and quickly ran back to her mother, who was chatting with another woman a bit further away. The little girl briefly turned back to Bennet. Her eyes sought his. He nodded appreciatively to her, and she gave a shy smile before hiding behind her mother.

The teenagers were in a party mood, fueled by alcohol. Two of them caught Bennet's eye as they stumbled through the neglected garden and discovered a portable environmental monitor. One grinned broadly, picked up the device, and let it fall onto the paved garden path with a loud bang, the metal parts striking the stone surface hard. He kicked the broken monitor over to his friend.

Bennet watched the scene with a heavy heart. The second boy, clearly drunk, swayed slightly and shouted with a broad grin, "What was that about Maroon? Anyone outside drops dead on the spot?" His slurred voice sounded mocking, as if the bleak times were long forgotten.

The first boy held his hand like a microphone in front of his mouth and imitated the voice of journalist Maria Cruz: "Not immediately, but the damage is irreversible." Then he licked his other hand and dramatically smoothed his hair, which made his friend burst into roaring laughter.

The two teenagers kept bellowing, without realizing that they were destroying the very device that was supposed to protect them from the consequences of their own negligence. Their indifference to the warnings they should have heeded was obvious. Freed from constant monitoring, they indulged in a frenzy of freedom and forgetting. They took turns kicking the broken monitor across the square, the metallic clatter drowned out by their laughter.

As Bennet turned to go home, he couldn't shake the terrible sound of metal scraping over cobblestones from his ears.

Clara Zheng was also out enjoying the city, and a smile appeared on her lips as she wandered along the sidewalk. It had been a long time since she had felt so light—as if the burden of the Gray Winter had finally fallen from her shoulders. She was happy to have left the office behind and appreciated the rare feeling of simply strolling through Plainfield—the Plainfield whose air she had helped to clean. Finally, people could breathe deeply again, and that was partly thanks to her. The sun's rays warmed her face, and the gentle wind played with her bun. Despite the harmony, she felt an indefinite unease rising within her.

Then she noticed it: more and more people recognized her. Clara felt their gazes, the gentle nods, the fleeting, grateful smiles as they walked past her. Was that an admiring look or something else? Unintentionally, something tightened in her chest. She turned away and looked into a shop window. Her own reflection stared back at her—the flawless image of the savior whose name was known everywhere. However, there was something strange in her eyes, something she didn't understand.

Behind her, in the reflection, she noticed movement. A man.

A gray coat.

Her breathing quickened, and her pulse raced. *He's here.*

She whirled around. Her heart threatened to skip a beat, but then she calmed. It was not the man she feared, just an older gentleman looking at her with friendly eyes, accompanied by a woman.

"Ms. Zheng, right?" he said, linking arms with the woman and smiling warmly. "It really is you. We wanted to thank you. You gave us our lives back."

Clara nodded, forcing herself to smile. "I'm glad I could help." The words slipped from her lips as if by themselves, but deep inside, she felt something harden inexorably. For a moment, she felt relief, but it vanished immediately. More people approached her with grateful words and friendly gestures.

She heard the voices only muffled, as if they came from afar. Clara felt like an actress on a stage, trapped in the spotlight. By now, she was surrounded, caught in a wave of recognition.

For a moment, she actually felt proud. Her technology had saved all these people. She had given life back to the world. Suddenly, however, a wave of anxiety overwhelmed her. *What if they find out the truth?*

At the edge of her field of vision, a shadow suddenly appeared. Behind a tree on the other side of the street—the gray coat.

Clara's breath caught, and cold sweat broke out on her forehead. "Excuse me," she muttered absently as she pushed through the crowd that had formed around her. Her steps became faster; the air suddenly seemed thicker, heavier. *The gray coat. He was there. I saw him. Has he come just to watch me, or does he finally want to confront me?*

"Stop following me," she blurted out as she rounded the tree, her hands clenched into fists. "This is sick."

With a big step, she reached the other side of the tree—and stopped abruptly.

There was no man in a gray coat, only a little boy pressing tightly against the tree, his big eyes wide open. His cheeks were flushed, a shy smile forming around his lips. Clara blinked. He was playing hide and seek.

"What are you doing here?" she asked breathlessly, the words rushed. *How embarrassing!*

The boy just stared at her silently. "Mom!" he suddenly shouted, high-pitched and shrill. A woman quickly came running over from the playground. She looked at Clara questioningly, as if trying to understand what had happened.

"I'm sorry... I..." Clara began, but she couldn't form a complete sentence. Blood was rushing in her ears; her heart was beating far too fast. "I thought..." She shook her head, unable to finish the sentence. It had just been another illusion. The gray coat didn't exist. Not here. Not now. *I'm losing my mind.*

The mother gently pulled her son to her. "It's all right," she said softly. Her eyes then widened. "Aren't you Clara Zheng?"

Clara hesitated. The world around her seemed to blur, and for a moment she didn't know what to say. Slowly, she began to step backward while forcing another smile. "Yes, that's me," she finally whispered, the words barely audible. She just wanted to get away.

"Thank you, Ms. Zheng. You saved us all," the woman said as Clara hastily turned away and left the place as quickly as possible.

The words of thanks echoed in her head, mixed with a fear that wouldn't let go. The man in the gray coat didn't exist, but the shadow was there. Always. And deep inside, she knew she couldn't escape him.

CHAPTER 24
MARIA CRUZ –
HIDDEN GUILT

Maria pulled her coat tighter around herself as the cold wind swept down the streets. A long workday lay behind her, and although she loved her job, she yearned for the warmth of her apartment. A quiet evening, perhaps a glass of wine, a book—she could hardly wait to put the day to rest. Her apartment building, an old brick structure, came into view. She exhaled in relief.

But as she crossed the street and reached the entrance, she abruptly stopped. A man stood there, little more than a shadow in the twilight. His gray coat shimmered dully in the faint light of the streetlights. He was tall, his hat pulled low over his face so that his eyes remained in darkness.

"Ms. Cruz?" His calm voice was the only sound on this quiet evening. "Do you have a moment? I have information that might interest you."

Maria straightened up. Her journalistic curiosity awoke immediately, but an uneasy feeling spread in her chest. "What's this about?"

"It's about Clara Zheng," he said. The name made her perk up instantly. "I think this information could change your career."

Clara Zheng. Now he had Maria's full attention. The heroine, the woman who had ended the Gray Winter and saved the world with her technology. *What can this man know that I don't already?*

Maria frowned. "We could talk in a café. There's one nearby..."

"The information is too sensitive to discuss in public," he responded calmly. "It would be better if we spoke somewhere we won't be disturbed."

Maria hesitated. Her instincts warned her that it would be wiser to dismiss him and simply walk away, but her curiosity was too strong—the prospect of something big that could change her journalistic career. She examined the man more closely, trying to see behind the facade of the gray coat. *He doesn't look like a criminal, at least not at first glance. How can I be sure he's not dangerous?* Her eyes searched for clues. The man appeared unarmed; his posture was relaxed, his voice calm and controlled, yet she couldn't shake the unease. She weighed her options internally. *Maybe I'm crazy, but I have to know what he has to say.* "Okay," she finally said as she unlocked the entrance door. "We can talk upstairs in my apartment."

The clicking of her heels echoed through the empty stairwell as they took the elevator to the top floor. The man remained silent, and Maria avoided looking directly at him. Instead, she let her gaze fall on his shoes—immaculately polished, clean, and neat. Oddly, she found them reassuring. *Well-kept shoes don't fit someone who poses an immediate threat.* She felt her tension ease.

Finally, she unlocked the door to her apartment and invited the man in. She still didn't know if she could trust him, but something about his calm, reserved manner drew her in.

Maria went to the kitchen to make coffee while her thoughts swirled with a thousand questions. Out of the corner of her eye, she watched as he slowly removed his hat and sat down on the sofa. His movements had something eerie about them, almost robotic, as if each gesture was carefully rehearsed, and his composure stood in stark contrast to the unrest spreading within her. It was as if he was following steps described in a script while she tried to understand the role she was supposed to play in this drama.

When she returned with two cups of coffee, she saw him pulling a newspaper out of his simple tote bag. She set down the cups, and he handed her the yellowed paper.

Maria accepted it hesitantly and first glanced at the date. The newspaper was from the year 2030. It was 17 years old. She didn't yet grasp where this was leading, but the picture on the front page made her blood freeze in her veins.

She blinked, unsure of what exactly she was seeing—it was blurry, dark, like a nightmare in black and white. At first glance, it resembled shadows, but the longer she looked, the more the outlines emerged. People. Burned, charred bodies, small bodies... they were children, their faces frozen in an agonizing scream.

A shiver ran down her spine, and her stomach turned. Her hands trembled slightly as she held the newspaper, unable to tear her gaze away from the horrific image. "What... what is this?" she asked, her voice choked with horror.

The man took a deep breath, as if he needed to collect himself. "This is the result of a failed experiment. The children... they were in the wrong place at the wrong time. Their presence wasn't planned, and it became their doom."

Maria swallowed hard. "What does this have to do with Clara Zheng?"

He looked at her for a long time, his eyes cold and empty. "It was her experiment. She and her team were eager to test their new technology. The goal was to neutralize particles in the atmosphere that were harming the environment. But the technology was far from mature. They chose a remote mountain region without thoroughly checking who might also be there. Had they researched better, they would have learned that a school class had set up camp there."

He paused for a moment, his eyes piercing hers. "Whether Clara knew the children were there or not, I can't say, but finding that out is your job as a journalist, isn't it? At the very least, she accepted the risk." His voice was calm, but the words seemed to grow heavier as he said them.

Maria felt her throat tighten, and she remained silent. The

man leaned forward slightly. "In any case, Clara and her team had everything prepared. But the radiation was unstable, unpredictable. When they started the test, the invisible wave hit the poor students who happened to be nearby. The children had no chance. They died instantly."

His attention wandered to the newspaper in her hands. "When they were found, their bodies were already burned by the radiation."

Maria shook her head in disbelief. "This never came to public attention? There were no reports about it?"

The man in the gray suit raised an eyebrow and nodded toward the newspaper she was still holding. "It did come to public attention—but not the truth." He pointed to the article's headline: *School Class Dies for Unexplained Reasons.* "They never found anything and eventually dismissed it as a weather phenomenon, an unexpected natural event. What nonsense! They probably never searched thoroughly either. The police wanted to close the investigation."

Maria let her gaze glide over the headline, which now seemed as empty as the man's eyes before her. She looked directly at him. "And you know the truth?"

"I worked for Clara back then," the man began, watching her closely. "The company wasn't called InnoTech at the time. She probably wanted to start afresh with the new name to leave behind what had happened. I wasn't directly involved in the project, but by chance, I found out everything. Of course, I left the company immediately afterward."

Maria looked at her hands and noticed how her knuckles stood out white as she clutched the thin paper tightly. "Those are very serious accusations," she said quietly, her eyes fixed on the image in the newspaper. "Do you have proof?"

The man remained calm. With a smooth movement, he reached into his tote bag again and pulled out a page that had apparently been torn from a notebook. It was protected in a transparent plastic sleeve. "This comes from Clara's lab journal at the time. It contains the records of the test, including the location and exact time. That's Clara's handwriting—you can have a forensic handwriting analysis done if you have doubts."

Maria placed the newspaper on the table and accepted the sleeve. With trembling hands, she studied the well-preserved page. She didn't understand many of the technical details, but figures on the different radiation doses caught her eye. Below that, the test location and date were recorded.

Her eyes widened as she took the newspaper in hand again. She compared the data—the time and place. It matched. Every detail fit seamlessly together.

A knot formed in her stomach. The test, the accident... it was all real. The evidence was convincing.

Maria looked at the man with narrowed eyes as she clutched the sleeve tightly. "Why me? What do you want from me?" Her voice sounded sharper, more impatient. She already knew the answer but wanted confirmation.

The man in the gray suit took his time responding, his cool eyes boring into her. "Because you have the platform to reveal the truth. People trust you. You're known for your integrity and for not being afraid to bring uncomfortable truths to light. It has to be someone the people believe, and someone who comes from Plainfield."

He leaned back, his face calm again. "You're the only one who can take this on."

Maria fixed him with a sharp gaze. "What happened to the other people involved? Clara didn't act alone."

"No, she wasn't alone. Her core team knew, of course. Two team members disappeared soon afterward. They probably couldn't cope with the guilt. Only Dr. Hansen is still by Clara's side."

Dr. Hansen—that's the likable chemist with the tousled hair whom I interviewed recently.

She stared at the man for a while before finally asking, "Who are you, anyway?"

He hesitated, then slowly raised his hands, palms up, as if to suggest it didn't matter. "Who I am doesn't change what happened," he said with a smile that seemed almost apologetic. "I'm just someone who knows the truth—and who has stayed silent for too long."

The man got up and smoothed his coat. "It's time," he said quietly. "You now know the truth. It's up to you to bring it to light."

Maria stood up, her thoughts racing. The evidence seemed irrefutable, and the tragedy was too great to ignore. But what would happen if she published the story? *Am I ready to turn the world against Clara Zheng?*

She gave a brief nod, and the man seemed to accept this as confirmation. He opened the door and said, "Then I wish you much success. It won't be easy, but I'm sure you already know that."

Maria stood motionless as the door closed behind the man. Her fingers still clutched the documents, but a clear realization settled in her mind: This would change everything—her career, her life. This was the biggest story she had ever held in her hands. Such a revelation would not only shake Clara Zheng but also the world's image of her.

This is it, she thought, her heart beating faster. *This will turn my career upside down. No other story comes close.*

For a moment, she felt the weight of responsibility, but then she felt determination rising within her. She had no more doubts. The truth had to come out.

Without hesitation, she sat down at her laptop. It was time to begin the research.

The next morning, Maria woke up just before noon. After researching into the early hours, images of the burned schoolchildren had haunted her sleep. The investigations into what had happened had lasted only a few weeks; the files were incomplete, and the trail led nowhere.

They probably couldn't make sense of the radiation damage back then. Where would it have come from? A UFO? A leak in a decommissioned nuclear reactor? The weather phenomenon explanation probably seemed more plausible. She snorted bitterly. *After all, the whole thing was localized to that one mountain region.*

Maria stared at the blank page on the screen before she finally straightened up. Perhaps the local police station in the mountains could help her. Determined, she grabbed her mobile phone and dialed the number. After several rings, a woman answered.

"This is Maria Cruz, journalist. I'm researching a case from the year 2030. It's about the school class that died in your region due to an alleged weather phenomenon. I'd like to speak with the lead investigator from back then."

"Let me check..." The voice on the other end sounded thoughtful, and Maria could hear clicking sounds. After a moment of silence, there was a soft sigh. "The commissioner who led the investigation is unfortunately no longer here."

Maria raised her eyebrows. "Could you give me his number? I'd like to contact him. It's very important."

The woman on the phone swallowed audibly. "That won't be possible, Ms. Cruz. Commissioner Klepper passed away a few weeks ago. The Gray Winter..."

Maria sighed deeply, ran her hand through her hair, and felt a new wave of frustration wash over her. "Do you perhaps know anything about the case?" she asked desperately.

A soft laugh sounded on the other end of the line. "Me? Oh, I'm afraid not. Back then, I was ten years old." The operator seemed to hesitate briefly. "And honestly, I don't think there are any more records in the archive. Such things eventually expire, you know? The case was closed."

"A weather phenomenon doesn't cause radiation victims," Maria replied incredulously. "That doesn't make any sense."

The woman on the other end sounded confused. "Radiation? As far as I know, it was burn victims, but like I said, the case is so old. It's not really talked about anymore."

Maria closed her eyes and sank back into her chair. Another lead that led nowhere. "I understand. Thank you for your time." She hung up and stared at the phone in her hand for a while.

Enough. It's time to go on the offensive.

Maria opened her address book and looked for Clara's number. In recent weeks, they had worked together several times, and she even had Clara's direct line, along with the assurance that she could call anytime. Without hesitation, Maria picked up the phone and dialed the number.

"Clara Zheng speaking," a clear voice answered.

Maria took a deep breath, and her heart beat faster. "Hello, Ms. Zheng. This is Maria Cruz."

"Ms. Cruz! Nice to hear from you," Clara said, her voice sounding pleased. "Are you planning a new report?"

Maria hesitated for a moment. "I wish the circumstances were different. I need to talk to you about something important."

A brief pause ensued. "That sounds serious. What's it about?"

Without beating around the bush, Maria stated her concern: "It's about the school class that died in the mountains 17 years ago."

The silence on the other end of the line was almost palpable, as if it filled the space between them, stifling any response. "I... I don't understand," Clara finally replied. Her voice had lost its warmth.

"I've received information suggesting that an experiment by your team went wrong back then," Maria continued. "I'd like to give you the opportunity to comment."

Clara's lack of a response did not deter Maria. "I have a handwritten lab entry," she said calmly. "From you, Ms. Zheng. It describes the experiment. The region and date of the test are also noted. Everything. It's your handwriting—and I will have it forensically examined if you plan on denying it."

The silence on the other end stretched painfully long until finally a soft sob was heard. Clara Zheng spoke with a trembling voice. "It was never my intention to hurt anyone... I never wanted that to happen."

Maria felt a chill rise within her. "So, you admit it?"

"It was... a mistake, a terrible mistake," Clara finally confessed. "The experiment turned out to be a complete failure. The radiation was extremely unstable, unpredictable. We only learned about the children through the press." Clara's voice broke off, and Maria could hear her trying hard to maintain her composure. "I didn't know they were there. It was... a nightmare—our guilt."

Maria took a deep breath. "And then you just covered it up."

"No one asked us any questions," Clara whispered. "I

immediately stopped the project and destroyed everything related to it."

"But you never made your culpability public," Maria said sharply. "You watched as the world dismissed the deaths of those children as a trivial weather phenomenon."

Clara responded only with a stifled sob. "I couldn't. I've built my life based on doing good. I wanted to improve the world. I *have* improved the world, but that incident... it would have destroyed everything. I... I didn't know how to tell people. We just kept quiet and let the police do their work."

Maria sat motionless, too perplexed to say anything.

"Will you publish it?" Clara's voice sounded broken, as if she already knew the answer but still didn't want to give up.

Maria hesitated for a moment. She felt the weight of the decision pressing on her shoulders. Then she straightened up and said with a firm, resolute voice, "Yes. It's my duty."

There was a long silence on the other end of the line. Maria expected Clara to beg her not to do it, to offer her money, but nothing of the sort happened. "Then so be it," Clara finally said. Her voice was now more composed. "It was my mistake."

Without another word, Clara hung up. The conversation was over, but Maria's thoughts were not. The truth now lay in her hands.

Maria spent the rest of the afternoon in front of her laptop. She stared at the blank page; the words simply wouldn't flow. Every time she tried to write, the events of the past hours echoed in her head. She closed her eyes and took a deep breath, but the thoughts wouldn't leave her. Finally, as dusk set in, she knew she had to make a decision. The weight of Clara's confession pressed heavily on her. She knew that the truth would unleash a storm. *What if this storm destroys more than it reveals?* Maria ran her hand through her hair as her thoughts whirled incessantly. Doubts gnawed at her; she felt torn between her duty as a journalist and her responsibility to society.

Then there was a knock at the door, and Mikael entered in a good mood. His smile faded, however, when he saw Maria's worried face. "Maria, what's wrong? You look totally exhausted."

She pressed her lips together. "Please, sit down." Slowly and with faltering voice, she told him everything—from the visit of the mysterious man to her fruitless research, then the conversation with Clara, the guilt she had admitted, and the evidence now lying before them on the table.

Mikael listened attentively and with a serious expression. His eyes grew darker. When Maria finished, there was silence for a moment.; Mikael seemed to be processing her words. Then he looked directly into her eyes and spoke firmly. "You absolutely have to publish this. People have a right to the truth. They need to know who Clara really is, what she has done."

Maria sighed and looked down. "I understand what you mean, but... I've thought about it a lot. The children are dead, and nothing we do will bring them back. And Clara... Clara will undoubtedly have to live with this guilt for the rest of her life. She is truly sorry. I believe she never wanted anyone to get hurt."

Mikael jumped up and paced restlessly around the room. "That doesn't change what she did. She covered it up, Maria! She lied to the world and let the children down. The world sees her as a heroine, while the families of the victims never got justice."

Maria looked at him, feeling the pain and anger in his words, then slowly shook her head. "She is a heroine! She saved the world, Mikael. Without her, we might not be here at all. Don't forget that! Okay, she made a huge mistake, but she'll have to deal with her own demons. Revealing this story would only bring destruction. If I publish the truth, it will be a scandal—but what good will it really do?"

Mikael stopped and looked at Maria intently. His gaze was hard, as if he were struggling with himself. "It's not just about a scandal. It's about responsibility. Clara made a serious mistake, and she has to face the consequences. People have a right to know the truth, no matter how painful it is. If we start hiding the truth, where do we draw the line? Don't we then betray our own principles? Your principles, Maria. You're a journalist. Uncovering the truth is your duty."

Maria blinked several times to hide the tears welling up. Her voice trembled as she whispered, "I know you're right. But what would be the consequence? People wouldn't just hate Clara, they would question everything she has achieved. They might even reject the new technology out of fear, out of mistrust. The world is too fragile, Mikael. A single misstep could destroy everything. I can't take that risk. The truth wouldn't create a better world—just chaos. And sometimes the truth is more devastating than we can imagine."

The words hung heavily in the room, and an uneasy silence spread between them.

"No, Maria," Mikael finally said, shaking his head sadly. "I thought we shared the same values, the same convictions. But if you're willing to sacrifice your principles..."

Maria's heart tightened. Was she about to risk everything? But the fear of the possible consequences of publication outweighed those arguments. "I've made my decision. I won't publish it. The truth won't die just because we don't reveal it now. There's nothing the world could learn from this revelation," Maria said resolutely.

She stood up, stepped toward him, and gently took his face in both hands. Her voice was soft but firm. "People need a heroine, someone they can believe in. And that takes precedence over truth."

When he finally looked at her, she recognized something that deeply frightened her: disappointment, perhaps even contempt. His gaze reflected the principles she had once admired so much in him—his uncompromising nature, his unwavering dedication to what was right. Now she realized that she had not only lost his approval but also his respect. He no longer saw her as an equal partner but as someone who had betrayed her convictions.

CHAPTER 25
HANNAH KOWALKSI –
THE BITTER TRUTH

On that sweltering hot day when the city was celebrating the government's grand festival, Hannah sat in her stuffy office at the institute, deeply engrossed in analyzing her stress test results of the membrane. Beads of sweat glistened on her forehead, but she ignored the heat. Her eyes narrowed as she stared at the results. "Oh, no..." she whispered in horror.

For weeks, she had suspected that the catalysts in the membranes, which were supposed to convert pollutants into harmless substances, were not as robust as they seemed. Data from the city showed that the membranes quickly reached their limits when pollutant levels in the air spiked suddenly. Hannah suspected this would lead to a blockage of the catalysts. She had assumed this overload was temporary and that the catalysts' function would soon normalize—at least, the air quality data showed stabilization.

It was only when reanalyzing the data that she searched for the expected end products like nitrate salts and zinc sulfites that functioning catalysts should have produced. She found these substances to be missing. That was the proof—the catalysts had failed. Even worse was the discovery that pollutants were accumulating in the membrane until it broke under pressure during the stress test, abruptly releasing the bound pollutants.

Now the reason for the delayed pollutant absorption was clear. It wasn't due to a short-term overload of the catalysts, it came because there was a delay in the pollutants being absorbed and bound into the membrane. The catalysts had long been blocked. The improved air quality shown by the monitors was an illusion. In reality, pollutants were accumulating unnoticed, and the membrane was merely serving as a barrier until it would eventually break.

Panic rose within her. How could this have been overlooked? The short-term successes had deceived everyone—the membrane had cleaned the air, but the catalysts that were supposed to cause the decomposition of pollutants had long since failed. Now the question loomed: How much longer until the membranes collapsed under the load of accumulated toxins and triggered a catastrophe?

The sounds of the festival outside formed a surreal backdrop to her grim discovery. When she opened the window, music, laughter, and the shouts of revelers streamed in—a joyful cacophony that stood in stark contrast to the imminent threat she had just become aware of. The carefree atmosphere outside underscored the oppressive reality reigning in her office.

Hannah wrinkled her nose. Amid the festive smells of grilled sausages and sweet treats mingled the sharp odor of exhaust fumes and diesel. Life was in full swing outside. Colorful garlands hung from the trees, string lights adorned the streetlights, and people danced exuberantly to the sounds of the live band on the main stage. Children ran around laughing, balloons in their hands—all while an unseen danger was brewing above them.

Completely unexpectedly, a heavy downpour began, drowning out the festivities. The rain, heavy and oppressive, made the hot asphalt steam. A biting, acidic smell rose, and Hannah froze. Acid rain! Could the membranes, soaked with pollutants, withstand the acid rain, or would they break under this load? Her hands began to shake; she clung to the table.

The stench of wet sulfur wafted into her office. Horrified, Hannah continued watching the rain outside, when suddenly a piercing beeping sound snapped her out of her thoughts. Frantically, she turned to the monitors, which were indicating an alarming deterioration in air quality. All signal lights were flashing red, and every single one was giving an alarm. Her heart raced, and adrenaline surged through her veins—the current air quality data was catastrophic.

"This is it," she whispered in horror. The membranes were collapsing. She didn't know how long ago the catalysts had failed, but the longer it was, the more pollutants had accumulated unnoticed in the membrane layers. Now, as the membranes broke down, the accumulated pollutants were abruptly released. Within minutes, an uncontrollable chain reaction unfolded— exactly what she had feared was happening.

Outside, the rain was discoloring; toxic streaks drifted through the air as the membranes continued to disintegrate. The stench became unbearable, and Hannah felt a burning in her lungs with each breath. A yellow-orange shimmer mixed into the rain—a sinister sign. This color could mean only one thing: highly toxic intermediates. The acid rain had reacted with the pollutants from the disintegrating membranes, triggering a dangerous chemical reaction. The membranes hadn't just failed; they had released a new, uncontrollable hazard that would spread quickly and have catastrophic consequences.

Hannah's hands shook as she glanced back and forth between the flashing warning lights and the discolored rain. Her thoughts raced; panic threatened to overwhelm her. The rain had become a harbinger of doom, the air more toxic than ever before. She had to act, but the weight of the situation paralyzed her.

With trembling fingers, she reached for the phone. Her heart pounded. She had to warn the government immediately.

But as she tried to dial the number, she felt a familiar numbness spreading in her fingers. *No, not now!* With all her strength, she painstakingly navigated through the phone. Finally, she reached the number of the Ministry of the Environment. With shaky breath, she pressed the call button; the dial tone sounded.

"We are currently unavailable. Please leave a message..."

"No, no, no!" Hannah screamed in despair. She let the phone fall onto the table. When it suddenly vibrated, she struck the device in anger with her elbow. Simon's name appeared on the display. She hesitated, then answered.

"Hannah!" he called breathlessly, as if he had run across the entire city. "You were right." The beeping warning signals in the background faded from her mind. She closed her eyes, her heart heavy.

"It's too late, Simon," she said quietly.

"I didn't want this... I didn't want to lose us." Simon's voice trembled, his desperate words almost pleading.

Hannah paused. Why now? She bit her lip, fighting against the burning sensation in her chest. "There was never an *us*. You chose the technology." Her voice carried the bitter tone of betrayal.

"I was wrong, Hannah. I thought the technology would save everything, but I was wrong—about everything. About the work, about you..." He hesitated, his voice now sounding softer, more vulnerable. "I didn't want it to end this way. I wanted to tell you that."

Hannah felt her chest tighten, but the emptiness inside her was overwhelming. An icy cold spread within her as she looked out onto the street. People were dancing, laughing, as if they didn't notice the toxic rain. "And now it's too late," she whispered, her words barely audible.

"I know, Hannah, I know! But I wanted to tell you so badly that I'm so sorry." Simon's voice was just a faint whisper, seeming to disappear into the distance.

"Simon..." She wanted to say more, but the droning of low-flying aircraft cut her off. Her gaze wandered outside, where a formation of planes left colored smoke trails in the gray sky, like luminous scars crisscrossing the city.

Her heart contracted painfully. *How can the government allow this? How can they just carry on as if nothing is happening?* Her fingers clenched around the phone; the situation was overwhelming. The shrill beeping of the alarm signals penetrated her consciousness again—loud and insistent, a sound impossible to ignore.

"It doesn't matter," she breathed in submission. The sight of the planes flying their routes undisturbed while the catastrophe escalated around them broke something within her. Without another word, she let the phone fall. The dull thud as it hit the floor sealed her final farewell to Simon.

Outside, people stared spellbound at the sky, as if this were a harmless show and not the beginning of their downfall. Her knees grew weak, and she had to lean against the windowsill. Anger, disappointment, and frustration welled up inside her. How could the government not only allow such blatant waste and environmental burden, but even promote it? How could this ignorance go unpunished—especially now, when every bit of progress was so fragile?

Tears burned in her eyes, not from sorrow but from pure rage. How could people be so blind to the reality so clearly before them? She turned around, her eyes fixed on the blinking warning lights on the monitors, which tirelessly spewed out their warnings—messages no one was willing to hear.

At that moment, a deep resignation overcame Hannah. It felt as if she were being pulled into a bottomless abyss. The weight of her realization that all the hard work and the risk to her health had been in vain pressed down on her like a ton of bricks. The stress had triggered her illness again—a painful reminder of the endless battles she had already endured.

She turned back to the window, gazing at the crowds dancing in the rain as if nothing in the world could be wrong—they laughed, cheered, utterly oblivious to the biting smell accompanying the acid rain. Some of them appeared puzzled, coughing or rubbing their eyes as the first toxic fumes reached their airways, but no one seemed to truly perceive the danger. A child stumbled, fell, and began to cry as it rubbed its eyes with wet hands, while a man next to him suddenly had a violent coughing fit. Yet the celebration continued—the people remained trapped in their ignorance, their unwavering belief in a world that no longer existed.

Children jumped into puddles as if they were harmless, while their parents watched with smiles. None of them noticed that the rain wetting their skin was toxic. The laughter, the exuberant shouts—all of it formed a stark, cruel contrast to the relentless alarms of the blinking monitors in the background, which confirmed Hannah's worst fears.

A bitter realization gripped her heart as Hannah understood that it was hopeless to fight against such overwhelming ignorance. The people she had worked so hard for seemed willing to accept their own destruction without the slightest resistance. A painful thought crossed her mind—perhaps it was time to leave humanity to its fate. In a world that so carelessly destroyed its own foundations of life, Hannah wondered for whom or what she was still fighting.

It was probably a gust of wind that slammed the office door shut with a loud bang. The biting stench of burnt rubber and metal wafted into the room through the open window, mixed with the rain, filling the air with an almost tangible toxicity. Hannah turned toward the door, her gaze sliding to the environmental monitor beside it. In that very moment, she knew that all hope was finally lost. The display glowed in a deep maroon.

EPILOGUE
THE SILENCE AFTER

The world as it once was had ceased to exist. Like a house of cards collapsing under the weight of its own arrogance, the cities had fallen, one after another, into eerie silence. The environmental monitor next to Hannah's office door tirelessly displayed maroon—the mute witness to a catastrophe unfolding inexorably. The technology that had once been celebrated as salvation had brought only temporary relief, for humanity had returned to its old, destructive habits until it had crossed the point of no return.

The cities, once full of life, now lay abandoned. Streets formerly bustling with crowds and cars were now covered by a thick layer of dust and toxins, which lay like a deceptive shroud over the remnants of civilization. The buildings, symbols of the brief upswing, stood empty and still, like monuments to human pride and ignorance.

Over the years, nature began to reclaim the abandoned places and cities. Plants sprouted from the cracks in the asphalt, and animals that had adapted to the new conditions roamed the ruins of human existence. However, this recovery was deceptive. It would take millennia to fully regenerate the damage humanity had left behind.

In this new world order, where humanity no longer existed, the planet slowly began to heal the wounds that had been inflicted upon it. Without the constant strain of industrial activities, without the incessant emissions and the waste that had suffocated the Earth for centuries, ecosystems were recovering. But it was a slow, arduous process in which the planet desperately tried to restore the lost balance.

Perhaps, in thousands or even millions of years, the Earth would once again be a place full of life and diversity, as it once had been before the era of human dominance. Perhaps new species would emerge from the ashes of the old world and fill the Earth with new life.

This was not the end but the beginning of a new chapter in the planet's long history—a chapter without humans, in which the Earth could finally breathe freely and renew itself without the shadow of human influence. In this silent, untouched world, the wind whispered stories of what once was—and of what could one day be again.

ABOUT THE AUTHOR

Martina Vieira, born in Bern and now living in the French-speaking part of Switzerland, finds a valuable balance in creative writing alongside her scientific work, which requires precision and accuracy. With her debut novel, *The Legacy of the Gray Winter*, published in 2024, she steps onto the literary stage.
For upcoming publications, you can search for her works on Amazon or sign up for her newsletter:
https://mailchi.mp/61fbaab30211/martinavieira.

www.ingramcontent.com/pod-product-compliance
Lightning Source LLC
Chambersburg PA
CBHW051608250726

48653CB00004BA/1404